You Can Be Amazing
Transform Your Life With Hypnosis

Also by Ursula James

Clinical Hypnosis Textbook:
A Guide for Practical Intervention

You Can Be Amazing

Transform Your Life With Hypnosis

Ursula James

CENTURY

Published by Century 2007

4 6 8 10 9 7 5 3

Copyright © Ursula James 2007

Ursula James has asserted her right under the
Copyright, Designs and Patents Act, 1988, to be identified
as the author of this work.

First published in Great Britain in 2007 by
Century
Random House, 20 Vauxhall Bridge Road,
London, SW1V 2SA

Addresses for companies within The Random House Group Limited
can be found at: www.randomhouse.co.uk/offices.htm

The Random House Group Limited Reg. No. 954009

A CIP catalogue record for this book
is available from the British Library

ISBN 9781846051975

The Random House Group Limited makes every effort to ensure
that the papers used in its books are made from trees that have
been legally sourced from well-managed and credibly certified
forests. Our paper procurement policy can be found at:
www.randomhouse.co.uk/paper.htm

Typeset by Roger Walker

Printed and bound in Slovenia by
MKT Print, Ljubljana

To Phil, my future husband and fellow dreamer

Acknowledgements

With love and thanks to my family for helping me believe that I can do anything I put my mind to.

With great respect to Nicola Ibison and the wonderful team at NCI Management for their constant support and effort, and to Luigi Bonomi for his quiet confidence.

With thanks to Hannah Black at Random House for making the whole process of writing this book so straightforward, and the lovely people at the Audio Workshop for making the recording of the CD so enjoyable.

And finally, my heartfelt gratitude to the wonderful people at Restful Change, Rick and Sue Sayer, for helping to keep me sane during the last year.

Contents

Dedication   v

Acknowledgements   vi

Preface   ix

1   Introduction to becoming amazing   1

2   Obstacles   26

3   Developing strength   47

4   Know what you want   68

5   Mind games   90

6   Motivation   111

7   Work out how to get it   132

8   Final preparations before the journey   156

9   Real life   175

10   The first step   194

Examples   215
  Weight control   217
  Relationships   218
  Running a marathon   219
  Career   220
  Fertility   222
  Writing a book   223
  Stopping smoking   224
  Learning a language   225

Useful Information   226

Preface

Eighteen months ago I was trapped in a role and with a life I hated, around people who drained me. I loved teaching and seeing clients, but in every other way I felt my life had gone up a blind alley. I was lonely, stressed (I drank too much and ate too late) and permanently tired. Now I have a new life, a beautiful mews house in central London, a home in France by the river, I drive the brand-new hybrid Lexus SUV, and I have just got engaged to a wonderful man. That's not all – in those eighteen months I have also published two books, got my own TV series and established three successful companies with my partner. Above all, I am healthy, balanced and happy, and I have more time to do the things that I enjoy than ever before.

What changed? How did I do this? Did I win the lottery? No. The only thing that changed was me. I finally decided to practise what I preached. You see, for the past ten years I have been teaching hypnosis to other people, and working one-on-one with my unique success programme to help them get rid of their problems and achieve their goals. So, instead of becoming resentful at their success, and getting more and more frustrated by my own lack of progress, I created 'You Can Be Amazing' and used hypnosis on myself – turning my life around completely.

You can do this too – you can get what you want out of life. In this book and the companion CD I have distilled the essence of 'You Can Be Amazing' – hypnosis for change. It's safe, easy and it works. However you wish to change your life – maybe you know what you want, maybe you are not completely sure, or you are just not happy with what you have – you can change your life and have it all. It's time to *be amazing*.

One warning: be careful what you wish for… you might just get it.

Enjoy the ride!

Chapter 1
Introduction to becoming amazing

If you want to transform your life into something special, this programme will stop you making excuses and give you the kick up the backside that you need to turn your life around.

So how do I set about becoming amazing?

Put simply, to *become amazing* you need three things:

- to know what you want
- success habits to take you there
- a good attitude to get you started

Annoyingly, without these three things in place, one of the following can happen. You might:

- start but not finish
- not start
- do everything right, but not be happy when you have done it all

Recognise any of these? If you do, there are sections in the programme to help you work through each of them individually. Within this programme I will spend time breaking each of these elements down so you will never make the same mistakes again and, more importantly, you will know what to do in future.

I will use hypnotic suggestions in the book, and the CD, and through the tasks which you will complete as you go on. Don't worry about what hypnosis is and what it does for the moment, I will explain that as we go. In fact, I will explain how each section will work for you as you work through the programme.

Hypnosis is a unique state of attention, one in which you put your thoughts in order, to get what you want *without ever tricking yourself out of it again*. You have probably experienced hypnosis before – when driving a car down a familiar road on 'auto-pilot', or when you have been really absorbed in a piece of music or a movie, and you stopped noticing what was around you. Hypnosis lets you cut out the distractions and concentrate fully on one subject. Hypnosis is safe, effective and, most important, controlled by you alone. No one can make you do anything you don't want to do. In addition, the hypnosis in this programme will act as an amplifier, taking all the things that you already know you want to do, and should be doing to achieve your goal. I will use hypnotic suggestions in the book, the CD, and the tasks which you will complete as you go on. I will explain how each section will work for you as you work through the programme. You will also be prompted exactly how and when to listen to the hypnosis CD tracks.

I will start with helping you get your goals and your dreams sorted out. I may as well tell you now that sometimes we get this bit very wrong. The thing we think we want maybe isn't really right for us at all, and we end up setting duff goals which our unconscious mind will interfere with because it knows the goal won't give us what we think it will. This is a form of self-sabotage – but more about that later. I am going to make this process so clear and easy for you, you won't really notice it happening until you start seeing the results. So, before going any further, you need to be really clear on the following:

- Do you know what you really want out of life?
- Is there a real benefit for you in achieving it?
- Will this goal AMAZE?

During the programme I will guide you through each of the steps you will take so it will be simple and straightforward. I will break down each of your stumbling blocks so you will be really clear on any of the tricks you used to play on yourself – and I will help you find ways of making sure that you don't trick yourself out of success this time. I will then use the audio-hypnosis part of the programme to 'fix' each section into your mind, and programme *out* of your mind any of the reasons for failing to succeed.

So, before you run off and start the process you will be properly prepared, and you will know:

- what you want
- how you are going to get it
- when you are going to start

Each element of the programme will use hypnosis to encode the appropriate suggestions in your mind, section by section, so success will become an unconscious habit for you – like driving or writing. When you drive a car, for example, you don't think about how you are driving that car. It just becomes something you do automatically. You no longer need to know exactly *how* you are doing it because the knowledge has become *unconscious*. This programme will use that part of your mind to make success into a habit. A habit that you will first learn consciously and deliberately, as you're working your way through the programme. Then it will move on to an unconscious level – little by little, so you won't need to think about your new behaviours, they will just become success habits, done without thought. The real joy of this process is it allows you to learn from your mistakes as well as your successes, in a way that tailors the programme to you and your requirements. Using this programme you will become one of those people you used to envy – confident, successful and enthusiastic about life.

What does it mean to 'be amazing'?

'Be Amazing' is a way of transforming yourself, your relationships, your career – your life. Some people already know this secret – they are the successful ones. These are people who seem to know how to **deal with anything, anybody, any situation** and to turn it to their advantage. They are also charismatic, exciting and good fun to be around. You too can be like this. We all have this potential.

So why aren't we all like that already?
Well, there are different reasons for each of us:

- childhood attitudes and beliefs
- the life you live now
- simple excuses – we are too lazy or too scared of what might happen when we take steps to change

I am also going to take you through how to deal with other people and their new reactions to you as you change, and when you have changed. Some people around you may have preferred you as you were, and will try to sabotage your change.

> **EXAMPLE**
> *Tanya was very overweight. I taught her the 'Be Amazing' programme, and the pounds fell away. Her partner, however, got more and more unhappy as* >>

> *she lost weight. In the end, he came to see me, as their arguments became so bad, she threatened to leave him. He was afraid that as she lost weight and felt more attractive, she would no longer want him. He had not discussed his fears with Tanya.*

In that example, because the couple were not communicating with each other, one became afraid as the other changed. It is really key to your success with the programme that you understand how it will impact on other people around you as you change, and there is a section later in which I go through with you precisely how to deal with this, and when to accept that some other people are just not healthy to be around – in fact, they can be toxic.

'Be Amazing' boils down to taking the life you have, and turning it into the life you want. To do this I use hypnotic suggestions to help you to reprogramme your mind. I don't do anything to you – you do it all – but the hypnosis puts the knowledge into the part of your mind where it can get to work automatically – without thought or effort from you. The 'Be Amazing' programme helps you get what you want out of life and changes your attitude to how you will get (and keep) it. It uses the power of your own mind, amplified by hypnosis, to do this safely, realistically and permanently.

Hypnosis can sound quite scary until you recognise that you are already making suggestions to yourself every day – but the irony is these are mostly negative ones. Significantly, the difference between the random suggestions made by you to yourself (and other people) on a daily basis and those made in hypnosis is that when you are in hypnosis you will be focused on

> **EXAMPLES**
> *I can't learn to ski.*
> *I couldn't start my own business.*
> *I can't go to the gym tonight.*
> *I can't go out without having a drink.*

the suggestions, so that only the ones which you *want* to take on board will 'fix' in your unconscious where you can then act upon them. When suggestions are made to you out of hypnosis, you most often don't even register them. These suggestions can be damaging. The suggestions made to you in hypnosis *cannot*. You will only accept suggestions in hypnosis that will be useful and realistic for you. This is why we spend time in the programme clarifying and refining the suggestions which you are going to make to yourself during the audio part of the programme, so you can be absolutely sure that these are the suggestions you want to hear.

As you work your way through the programme you will notice whenever you are giving yourself a negative suggestion, and you will find yourself looking for, and finding the word, 'can' instead of 'can't', 'will' instead of 'won't'. This will take time, but it will come, and when it does you will find the world of opportunities opening up before you.

The hypnotic suggestions in 'Be Amazing' will only work to your advantage – they are designed to be safe, manageable, and driven by you. 'Be Amazing' is unique in that once you have worked your way through it, you will have achieved your goal (be it giving up smoking, losing weight, changing jobs, resolving relationships, starting a new business, etc.) and also developed new, unconscious habits of success which will be yours – for ever. You will think differently, feel differently, act differently – but most importantly you will be able to begin to get the best out of your life, starting today.

OK, down to practicalities.

There are three sections:

- Know What You Want
- How to Get What You Want
- Get On With It

Each one of these is broken down into activities; some parts you just read, in some you make notes, others you listen to. You will find that some elements are more relevant to you and your goal than others, and you will pay attention to only what is relevant to you.

Each chapter is also broken up into small sections, and each section has a specific purpose. Complete the actions as you work through the book. Interestingly, the action of writing things down makes them more real, more concrete. Also, the activity of writing helps you make the mental connections which will be used in creating the *amazing you*.

What to do when you are asked to listen to hypnotic suggestions

In addition to reading and making notes, you will be asked to listen to specific tracks on the CD. As you do this, you can relax. No need to listen too hard, or to try to take the suggestions in. Just relax. When listening to the CD, if you suddenly need to pay attention to something, you will be fully awake. While listening you remain fully in control. If, however, you drift off to sleep, that will be fine also. You will remember as much as is important for you to remember. When you are listening to the CD tracks, do not attempt to do anything else. It is very important that you are concentrating only on what is being said to you. You will enjoy this part!

Just so you know, there are six tracks in total on the CD, and you will be prompted when to listen to each of them. The six tracks are:

- Confidence
- Amazing You
- Motivation
- Habits of Success
- Focus
- Get Started

You will be given clear instructions on what to do at each step in the book. You will also find that there will be some sections which you won't need to do because they don't apply to you, and you can skip through those. We all have our own stumbling blocks, and you will recognise which ones apply to you as you go through it.

How long is this going to take me?

The audio tracks are between ten and fifteen minutes long, so you will easily be able to find time to listen to them.

In terms of how long the programme takes to complete, well, if you sat down and worked your way through it the entire programme would take only a few hours to complete. However, you already know that you are not going to do that, nor is this programme designed to be digested in one big lump. 'Be Amazing' has been developed for real life, and it has been created so that you can do a section whenever you have ten minutes here or there to yourself. Do a little, often, and you are much more likely to succeed. Work through the programme in this way and you allow your unconscious mind the time it needs to **take in all of the suggestions appropriately**.

This hypnosis stuff all sounds very good, but what if I don't think that I am suggestible?

I have news for you: you are, we all are. We constantly make suggestions to ourselves and to other people, and others make suggestions to us – often unconsciously. It is very rare for a person to ask a straight question. When we want someone else to do something, we rarely tell them what we want them to do – we usually suggest, and within the suggestion we hope that they understand what we are trying to say. When someone asks, 'Would you like to sit down?' they don't actually mean 'Would you like to do this?' as the answer would be 'yes' or 'no'. When we ask this, we mean 'Sit down!' So remember, suggestions are a part of day-to-day communication. This programme will also train you to be more selective in the suggestions you take on board on a daily basis as well.

How we decide to respond to suggestions also depends on our relationship with that person. If we trust and feel comfortable with them we are much more likely to carry out the suggestion. This could be a problem when we make suggestions to ourselves (which is what you are going to do in the hypnosis section), as you need to trust and feel comfortable with yourself – and not everyone does. Don't worry, this is something we will work through in the programme, and if it is relevant to you, you will carry out the actions suggested, **start to trust your own judgement,** and **start to feel comfortable when you make positive suggestions to yourself** about how you are going to change. Believing in yourself is really important to becoming and remaining successful, and by the end of the programme this will be second nature to you.

Your mood will also affect how you choose to receive the suggestions. When **you are feeling positive**, you are more likely to accept positive suggestions. When you used to feel low, negative suggestions came into your mind and took hold. In this programme your state of mind will become positive first so that when the suggestions are given, you will **be comfortable to carry out the suggestions**.

When I make comments and suggestions in the book about ways to change your life, these suggestions will be reinforced by the hypnosis CD tracks. Only the ones which are relevant and useful to you will be taken on board by your unconscious mind. Don't try too hard as you read and do the tasks. You will soon learn that the hypnosis will guide you, unconsciously, to the best way of getting what you want out of this programme. **The hypnosis works much better when you just relax.**

How the programme works

The programme has been put together so that you will be able to see, hear and get to grips with this programme no matter how well you think you can learn. I bet you have songs in your brain that you don't remember learning – this is called unconscious learning and the programme works using this part of your mind. The best part about it is that you don't have to try to learn – it will sink in without you even being aware it is happening. Also, as most of the suggestions in the programme will go in unconsciously, you may not be aware that you are starting to do things differently, that you are changing.

Important note: you will only take on board suggestions that are right for you – and only positive suggestions at that. Because not everyone learns in the same way, this programme has been put together to make sure that you will be able to learn in your own way and your own time so that the changes stick. Some people need to see things, and be visually stimulated, then they can copy what they have seen. Some people need to listen, and once they hear suggestions can understand them fully and carry them out easily. Some people need to get hold of ideas – to feel these changes emotionally and physically to make them real. Whether you are a visual learner, auditory processor, need physical stimulation or all three, this programme will work for you. Each stage of the process is worked through in all three ways of processing information. These methods, called modalities, are all used in the programme – so you will get the optimum stimulation you need to *be amazing*.

Additionally, the suggestions in this programme are more than just words – they are designed to stimulate your imagination, your memory, and your emotions. This helps the learning 'stick' in such a way that the change comes without effort – unconsciously – and so, naturally to you. You will respond to the suggestions because they feel right to you, and you will **quickly start to notice the benefits**.

… First you will be given the picture.

By reading through the book you will start to visualise your goal-setting process. The book is written using the hypnotic language of suggestion, so you won't even notice when you are responding to suggestions. Some people need to see their goals to recognise that things are happening. Visual cues can be the look on someone's face when you tell them you no longer smoke, or the sight of yourself in a mirror when you have lost weight. Visual people need these types of suggestions to make their goals happen. This programme uses visually stimulating exercises and suggestions to create the images of success – and the action of reading stimulates this part of the brain. When you are reading, your eyes move from side to side (lateral eye movement), which is the same type of movement that occurs when you dream. When we dream we make connections all over the brain and we start to create all kinds of mental images – dreams. Through the physical activity of reading we are making the same movements which happen when we are imagining. So you can think of the act of reading as training your imagination – no matter what the reading material! People who are visual processors will benefit most from the reading part of the programme.

I see what you mean!

... Then you will get to hear all about it.

By listening to the companion CD you start to make auditory connections of success, and can start to hear and listen to yourself as you begin your positive self-talk.

Some people need to hear the sounds of success – for example, hearing someone tell you how good you look now you have lost all the weight. Auditory suggestions are made in the CD, and cues, such as the sound of a motivating voice, best help people who process information in this way. The auditory nature of the CD will supplement the written suggestions for these types of people and they will respond to this part of the programme best of all.

That sounds like a great idea!

...Finally you will get to grips with the programme.

The programme sets tasks where you start to feel the changes happening, and the positive emotions that are associated with getting the best from your life.

Some people need to 'feel' the changes happening to recognise that their goal is becoming a reality. These are 'hands-on' people, who benefit most from carrying out the activities suggested. An example would be feeling the shape and weight of the notebook which you wrote in. These people respond best to activities and notice the benefits of them more than any other group. By working with your hands, and more specifically by writing things down, you are strengthening connections from the peripheral nervous system back to the brain. This creates a bio-feedback system which in turn makes it easier to make more mental connections. An example of this working can be seen with children who learn to play a musical instrument – their language skills develop faster. These benefits of hands-on activity are due to the architecture of the brain – strengthening one set of connections has a direct impact on others.

I can handle that!

Most of us are a combination of all three – and that is why this programme is so successful. When one type of suggestion takes a back seat, other types can take over, so you are constantly motivated and stimulated. As you work through the programme you will notice that you respond better to some suggestions than others. That's fine, go with it, it just means some of the suggestions have tapped more easily into your natural modalities than others. It doesn't matter how the suggestions go in, only that when you have taken them on board, they feel natural and appropriate to you. This is why it will seem as if some of the suggestions are repeated. They are. This is to make sure you hear, see or feel the right suggestions at the appropriate times for you and in the correct way to make them work.

Hear it, see it, feel it happening!...

The 'Be Amazing' programme will work success into your life by activating small, but significant, changes to the way you do things. Added to this is the power of hypnosis to take what you want to do, and translate it into action – unconsciously. So without you even being aware of what is happening, you start to work towards your goals without conscious effort.

This book is about you – no one else. In here you will find only clear, practical advice. I have added examples of case studies only where they clarify a point. Once you have worked your way through *You Can Be Amazing* you will be well on the way to getting what you want and you will have a set of life tools that work for you whatever you set out to do in the future. And, if you are starting to wonder when the programme begins, **the change in the way you are thinking has already started...**

So what is so different here to anything I have tried before?

The programme's uniqueness is in these three elements:

1. By making the steps small and building them into your daily life without dramatic change, you don't even notice that you are changing.

2. The programme uses repetition of suggestions (written, heard, and through movement as you turn each page) so that what you do and how you do it helps the suggestions 'stick' in your unconscious mind, where they become habits and memories. This is called learning by rote – doing the same activity time and again until the neural pathways are strong enough so that you do the action without conscious thought.

3. It uses all of your senses to 'fix' the suggestions permanently into your mind – like a song that won't go away! This involves the brain in making biochemical changes which reinforce the new memories by associating them with emotions and images.

The book also includes tips and hints throughout to guide you and keep you firmly on track.

Finally, the main difference between this and any other programme is the way 'Be Amazing' uses hypnosis and auto-suggestion to make positive changes that are safe, practical and acceptable. No one is going to fool you into failure again, because the hypnosis part of the programme is going to give you everything you need to get on track to succeed – and stay there – no matter what happens. You will use the hypnosis tracks on the CD to enter hypnosis, where you can then make the suggestions you create in the programme to yourself. This auto-suggestion is what really makes the programme unique, because you are the unique variable. You create the suggestions – and because

you do, you will only give yourself suggestions that are
going to work for you.

What's in it for me?

I will tell you: *you can be amazing*. Put simply, if you follow
the programme you will create a better life – a much better
life. I know this to be true because I already know
something about you. If you were content with your life as
it is, you would not be reading this book. You might be fed
up with your job, or your relationship, your habits, your
body or your career. Whatever it is, I bet you that you have
probably read self-help books before because you really do
want to change things, and just want something simple
and practical that really works. Well, this is it. This is the
book that will change your mind, change your attitude,
change your life. What is in it for you is the life that you
want – the control you want – a new you with a better
future. What is in it for you is a new life, something to get
excited about – and it's about time, isn't it?

If, when you are reading these words, you are thinking
to yourself that it all sounds too good to be true, let me
tell you something straight. I have done this for myself and
for hundreds of other people already. I *know that this
works*. I have seen it transform people from bored, sad
underachievers to remarkable people – *amazing* people.
People you want to be around – people who are exciting

and interesting and – above all – fun to be with. People who often got so much more than they bargained for when they started to change.

Speaking for myself, I can honestly say that I was already brilliant before I did this programme. I was brilliant at fooling myself into thinking that I shouldn't even try to do more with my life, and I couldn't achieve it if I did try. With that attitude no wonder I failed to achieve! There is such a thing as a self-fulfilling prophecy, where we end up getting the very thing we dreaded. You know why? Because we *make* it happen. We look out for it, we listen out for it, and eventually we find it. You are already creating your future by doing this – why not use this ability to predict a brilliant future, instead of a dull one?

Apart from people who are already successful, the only people you will meet who change their lives as dramatically as you are about to are people who have had a brush with death. It's incredible how nearly dying makes you start living – and getting as much out of life as you can. *You Can Be Amazing* – and start living now.

A warning though – not everyone is going to appreciate the new you. Some people will want you to go back to the way you were before. Predicting how some of the people around you will react when you do change, and knowing how to deal with them when you have is really important in making sure that the changes become permanent. That is why there is a whole section called 'Complainers and sustainers' later on in the book.

In this programme you will find, understand and start using the three basic components to changing your life. The first one is getting to grips with your goal – the 'what do I *really* want out of it?' part. The second are the steps you need to take to get it – the habits, if you like. The final component is the foundation stone to it all – the first small step that you will take to start the change. So, that's what's in it for you: a new life, and the confidence to live it to the full. There is another part to that question though – '*what's in it for you to change?*' You see, some people – and we will find out later on if you fit into this category – are very good at explaining *why* their life is arranged the way it currently is. These are the people who are able to explain all the reasons why they smoke, why they are overweight, and why they haven't yet got around to sorting out their lives. Ironically, these are often the people who are really good at sorting out *other* people's problems while unable to deal with their own.

When I work one-on-one with people who come to me to *be amazing*, some of them tell me that they want to change – and then go on to tell me all the reasons *why* they do things the way they do. So I completely understand about being in two minds when it comes to change and how frustrating that can be. People who talk this way *do* want to change, they *do* want success, but they have got so locked into justifying why they do things the way they do now, they find it difficult to step out of that box.

EXAMPLE

Mike is a smoker. He has a stressful job. He came to me to stop smoking, and then told me all the reasons why it was going to be difficult for him to stop. 'It helps me think, helps me relax, it is the only way of getting away from my desk.' I used hypnosis to help him understand that he was making excuses for not dealing with his underlying stress – so we dealt with this first, and he stopped smoking effortlessly.

You might need to work on 'being in two minds' and I will cover this in a later chapter.

By now you should be beginning to wonder when I will get on with it. When will I reveal the location of this holy grail of self-improvement? Not quite yet. You see, without you being aware of it, I am already making suggestions to you to help you change your way of thinking. Your ideas about yourself are already changing and you have already started the programme without being consciously aware of it.

What has been happening is, by telling you what the programme can do, by my *selling* to you the benefits of this change, you are starting to *want* to know what it is that will make it happen. You are getting curious now, and because you are getting interested, **you are also getting MOTIVATED**. You now want to know how to change. Each step in this programme is about changing your mind in small, subliminal ways. Your thoughts are starting to move on to what this programme can possibly do for you, so you have already started to change your mind about the possibility of change. Just a little more preparation, and then it will be time for you to start tailoring the programme so that it will work for you.

By the way, I will let you know when I am making suggestions to you, so that you remain in control throughout, and can decide whether you want to take them on board or not. There are suggestions all the way through the programme. You have probably already noticed that some of them are in bold. Read them again if you like – they are called embedded suggestions, and you have been taking them on board without even registering that you are doing so. This will happen because you are comfortable with the suggestions. If you really notice them, it is because your conscious mind is filtering the information first to decide whether the suggestion is right for you. Your conscious awareness will always be there to protect you from any suggestions which could be harmful or unrealistic, so you will always be safe and in control throughout the programme.

Know What You Want

Chapter 2
Obstacles

In the first chapter I introduced you to the basic system and idea behind the programme. From now on, I will give you instructions on *how* to make things happen for yourself. The book is split into sections which follow a repetitive format. This chapter deals with all the reasons why you may have had a problem setting a goal before. The purpose of this is to clear the way ahead before you start trying to make changes.

The next chapter will take you through all the resources you have in place to make it happen for you, and the purpose of this is to prime you for change. The one after that will tell you exactly how to make change happen. The goal-setting process will then be complete.

You will move on to the next section, which will **repeat the pattern**, but this time the subject will be success habits. Then you will be taken through the **same process** one final time, but this section will be about making the first step that sets the whole sequence of events in motion. It will all become clear as you work your way through it.

Why is the process so repetitive?

If you notice the repeating patterns and suggestions throughout the programme – good. Repetition is part of learning, and what you are doing is learning how to be successful. This is particularly important in making the hypnotic suggestions work. We learn most effectively in sets of three, so you may notice that when you hear or read or action a suggestion for the third time, your unconscious mind registers this, and thinks, 'Don't I know this already?' That is when the information sticks permanently. The more patterns and suggestions are repeated in the book, the CD and through the actions, the less conscious you will be of them, the less notice you will take of them, and the more easily they will sink into your unconscious mind without you engaging your conscious thoughts to analyse the process. It is essential that you do the 'actions' because these are your way of tailoring the programme to you. Some of them will seem more relevant than others, but it is worth doing them anyway because it will help you understand more about yourself, and give you a greater knowledge of how other people make changes. By doing the actions you are discovering how the programme is going to fit into your life, and how you are going to make it work best for you. They will very quickly start to become unconscious processes – without effort. Your unconscious mind will then start to personalise the suggestions to get what you want. Don't worry, all you have to do to *be amazing* is concentrate on what's in front of you, whether that is reading a section, listening to a CD track, or working through one of the actions. That's all. Nothing else matters in making this work for you. Just do one thing at a time and everything will fall into place.

This chapter focuses on the reasons why you have not got started before, so you can understand them, and make sure that you don't trip yourself up at the first hurdle. Obstacles are often made bigger in our mind when we don't feel confident. When we lack self-confidence, for whatever reason, it is easier to concentrate on all the obstacles and difficulties which we might come across if we do start changing, rather than focusing on how brilliant it is going to be when we get the life we want.

Looking at the world this way then becomes a habit, and we can find that we talk ourselves out of *becoming amazing* and getting the life we want before we even start. People become overwhelmed by the enormity of what *might* happen if they do get what they want. This is where the 'Be Amazing' programme really comes into its own. By breaking up the changes into small, manageable pieces you can, and will, get what you want out of it.

First of all, I will focus on helping you to understand what your own personal obstacles are. If you are somebody who has failed to get started in the past, then you will find the key to getting beyond this point in the next sections.

Self-sabotage

The main obstacle to change is yourself, and your attitudes. To assess whether you are your best friend or your own worst enemy, ask yourself these questions:

- Do I deserve a better life?
- Will I be able to deal with the impact of these changes?
- Do I really want to change?

For any change to happen and become a long-lasting change, you need to be able to say yes to each of these questions. If you cannot say yes, then you will not get started on this process, so the first thing I am going to do is to help you to change your mind about your potential. Let's go through the questions individually.

'Do I *deserve* a better life?' Some people don't feel that way at all. They may feel lacking in confidence, or have low self-esteem, and just don't get started on their ambitions because they feel they are doomed to fail. I have had many clients over the years who have had these issues – and changing these attitudes has been crucial to helping them change. If you are going to get a better life for yourself, you need first to believe that you are good enough, and capable enough, so that you deserve more. This is where hypnotherapy is in a league of its own. Even without any other form of suggestion, when hypnotherapy is used to help you feel better about yourself (ego-strengthening it is called), it can work miracles. People can literally change overnight. So, if your immediate response to the question *'Do I deserve a better life?'* was to say no, then you are going to pick up on the appropriate suggestions in the 'Confidence' CD track to work on this, and you will really notice a difference in how you feel about yourself. Others will notice it too! Don't worry about when to listen to the track, I will direct you, so you don't need to do anything at the moment. Recognising you deserve a better life and believing in yourself is key to long-lasting change. If you don't feel you deserve a better life you will keep on talking yourself out of it. When you do recognise you deserve more, **from this point in time nothing and no one will ever be able to distract or disturb you from getting your goal**.

EXAMPLE

Marion was a nurse. She was always doing things for others and putting them first. When I worked with her, she believed that this was her 'nature' and something that she couldn't change, and didn't really see the need to change. She believed that people liked her because she was always available to help, and wouldn't like her any more if she wasn't always there for them. When we had worked together for a while on building up her self-esteem, Marion admitted that she was often angry and resentful at the people >>

---

she was helping, because they were not there for her when she needed them. Once she grew in confidence, she recognised that she deserved more out of life and from her relationships with others. She started asking for help, and learned to say 'No' occasionally. Marion also left the partner she was with and is now in a new relationship; one which is mutually supportive and where she feels she can grow and develop as a person.

The second question, 'Will I be able to deal with the impact of these changes?', is an interesting one. First of all, we cannot accurately predict *how* someone else is going to react when we change. We can only imagine. When we imagine something that has not yet happened we base it on our memories, and how we believe they are going to react. This alone is often enough to stop some people from starting to *become amazing*. They talk themselves out of it because they decide that they don't want the hassle.

As before, you will find yourself paying attention to the relevant suggestions in the 'Confidence' CD. These are designed to help you stay in your own head, and not try to predict how other people are going to respond when you change. These suggestions will help you recognise that what you are trying to do is positive and beneficial for you. If the people around you don't like it, then you will recognise that it is their problem, not yours.

EXAMPLE

Kate was a single mum, fifty-two years old and had three adult children. She had focused all of her attention on her children while they were growing up, and had sacrificed her career to bring them up as best she could. Now they were grown up she wanted to go back to university and do an MBA, and after that, start up her own business. From the moment she told her children what she intended to do, her children's problems suddenly seemed to amplify. They had issues with their relationships, their jobs – and all of these problems were brought straight to Kate. At first, her instinct was to take over and sort the problems out, something her children were more than happy for her to do. At this point, she came to see me because she was starting to get stressed and tearful, and she was coming to the conclusion that she would have to give up on the MBA and her new career. Through the work we did, Kate soon recognised that her children were bringing the problems to her because of their fears that they were 'losing their mum', and that until Kate took a step back and allowed them to sort out their own problems (including making their own mistakes), she wasn't accepting them as adults. The work we did as part of the 'Be Amazing' programme helped her build stronger boundaries. She now has very good relationships with her children, and >>

when they do bring her their problems it is for her advice – not her intervention. She went on to gain her MBA and is now on the way to running her own business.

The third question, 'Do I really want to change?', sounds too obvious to be asked. Of course you want to change, you will say. However, if you take a step back, ask yourself: *'Is there a real and positive benefit **for me** to put in the effort to change?'* If you are trying to change to please someone else, or if you feel that you ought to, then I have news for you. You are going to keep finding reasons why you are not going to do it, and even if you do achieve it, it will not make you happy.

EXAMPLE

Alison was training to become a doctor. She was suffering from eczema, often felt stressed and was frequently ill – something that hadn't happened before she got into medical school. Although very intelligent and more than capable of passing the examinations, she also found that her grades were suffering. When I worked with Alison using the programme to get to the root of her problem, she recognised that she did not want to go into medicine – it was her parents' idea and she was doing it to $\gg$

please them. She felt that if she did not complete her training she would be letting them down.

After working through the programme, Alison went to talk to her parents and explained the situation to them – that the study was making her ill. Because of the way that 'Be Amazing' works, she was able to take not only a problem, but a solution to them. She told them not only what she didn't want – to become a doctor – but also what she did want out of life. Alison switched courses and is now studying to become a photographer. She is healthy, well balanced, and has a good relationship with her parents. At first they found her decision difficult to understand, but when she explained how she is now so much happier doing what she is doing, her parents became supportive as they genuinely only had her best interests at heart.

The goal has to belong to you; to be something you really want, something that will make you happy when you have achieved it. If you cannot find a real benefit in changing, then you will not change. Again, you will find that as you work your way through the programme your goal will become clearer to you, in fact, your goal will start *to amaze.*

You deserve more out of life. You can make your own decisions and will be able to deal with anything, anybody and any situation that is the result of changing your life.

This leads quite naturally on to the subject of guilt. I know that some of you, reading the last section, thought about how guilty you would feel in some of those situations. Interesting, isn't it? If you ever feel guilty when you do something for yourself, you need to realise that if you don't change the way you feel about yourself and your needs, your guilt will become a hurdle to progress. Until you realise that it is OK to do things purely for you, then you are not going to do it. The guilt will loom over you like a big cloud, and when (or if) you do achieve your goal, you will feel so guilty that you will not enjoy your success, and you will sabotage it.

Below is the first of your actions – tasks which I have set to help you tailor this programme to yourself. Do them as you go along, and be as honest as you can – it will make the whole process easier for you.

ACTION

Take ten minutes and write down all the things that you feel guilty about. Go through that list again, and *be honest with yourself*. Are you really responsible for all of them? If not, draw a line through ones that >>

you aren't responsible for. There are suggestions on the CD which will help you deal better with anything left on the list.

No one *makes* you feel guilty, you *choose* to respond in that way.
You will also find suggestions on the CD which will help you let go of inappropriate emotions and help you find better ways of responding to these situations, so there is no need for you to do anything except to be more aware of the situations you identified at this time. The more aware of them you become, the more you will be able to respond appropriately as you continue to *become amazing*.

It's got to be perfect

Ah, bless the perfectionists. I love them. They are the people who are better than anyone at fooling themselves into believing that they are doing everything that they can to get things right! They convince themselves that it is so important to do things 'properly' that they either end up doing nothing at all for fear that it won't be perfect, or stop when they feel that things are not going to plan.

Until you start recognising that it is OK to spend time and effort on doing the things that you may not get right first time, then you are not going to get started. Life is all about trial and error, and it is unlikely that you will get things right the first time. Be prepared to do things in a different way as soon as you realise that what you are doing is not working. Remember, if you flog a dead horse, all you will get is a tired arm. You will find suggestions in the 'Confidence' track on the CD to activate the changes you need to make. This will only happen (and the same applies to all of the suggestions) if this is one of your patterns.

To succeed you need to be flexible, and be prepared to make mistakes.

Clear your path

Whole books have been written on feng shui, and how important it is to clear the clutter. This section, as with every section in this book, is here because it is relevant to your success. There are two types of clutter: mental and physical. I will discuss mental clutter later in the chapter, but first I want to discuss physical clutter – the stuff we surround ourselves with on a day-to-day basis.

Let me ask you a question. When was the last time you cleared out your bedside or office drawers, or the bag you carry to work? If the answer is never, or not recently, it is time for an overhaul. I often ask female clients who find it difficult to move forward to empty out their handbag and show me what in there is directly relevant to their day. I asked one woman to do this and among all the accumulated dust at the bottom of the bag was a rectal thermometer! I asked her when was the last time she needed to use it, and she said she never used it. Her excuse for it being there was that she was a nurse, but she had forgotten that it was there! This is a classic case of how we can always find a reason to justify our actions. If you are carrying around things that are not useful for you, you will clog up your capacity to find things that are.

Travel light, and only take with you what is relevant to your purpose.

The contents of our bags, our cars, our offices and our homes are all a reflection of who we are and how we feel about ourselves. If our home is packed to the gills with objects, you will find that you only use a small proportion of the contents, and there will be things that you keep buying because you can't find the one you already have. When I started clearing out my home I found nine travel adaptors! This is an example from one of my clients: they had so much stuff that they could not bear anything more coming into the house, so they did not open their post, just let it pile up by the front door, unopened. The example is to show a knock-on effect of having too many possessions.

Now let me be clear on this, I am not saying that you need to get rid of everything you own, and only keep what is useful. But clearing out clutter – selling pieces, giving away to charity or freecycling (www.freecycle.org) them – and generally putting some order and structure into your living and working environment is a perfect way to prepare yourself to make changes. Not only does it help you to reduce stress, but it also helps you to let things go, mentally. So why don't people organise their environments into something which will work for them? There are a number of reasons:

Sentiment

'I can't get rid of that, my Auntie Beryl gave it to me.' I have heard so many variations on this theme over my years in practice. If you have something in your home, or your life, and you keep it simply because you loved the person who gave it to you, but you don't like the object itself – get rid of it. It does not mean that you have stopped loving that person.

'I can't get rid of that pair of trousers, I might fit into them again/they were very expensive.' Yes, you might fit into them again, but they will more than likely be out of fashion by then. When people hold on to clothes, they are usually trying to hold the feeling that wearing those clothes gave to them.

EXAMPLE

Jacqueline had a beautiful, expensive dress in her wardrobe. She had not worn it for ten years. Every time she looked at it she felt sad, because when she wore it she was trim and happy. I worked with Jacqueline to get her to recognise that what she wanted was the feelings back again, and that she >>

> *could get rid of the dress because seeing it made her feel sad, rather than motivated her to lose weight as she originally thought it would.*

If you keep hold of objects that have become a burden to you they will only weigh you down on your journey.

Comfort blankets

'I might need it.' If you haven't taken something out of a box since you moved house, or out of the cupboard since you put it there, do you really *need* it? Some people fill their space with all sorts of things they are afraid to get rid of because they feel more secure to have them. Spare buttons, manuals from electrical goods that they don't even have any more, drawers full of pens – the list could be never-ending. Surrounding yourself with things for the sake of it is like building a wall around you for protection. Do you really need it? When you feel confident in yourself, you will be ready and able to let these things go.

If you have boxes and boxes of photographs or letters from loved ones at home that you hardly ever look at, now is the time to sort them out. You can throw them away, or at least put some of them where you will appreciate them more. You are not discarding the memories that go with them – in fact, you are making room for the good memories to motivate you in future.

EXAMPLE

Patricia got divorced. When she moved into her new home she found that she had brought with her lots of photographs, and just pushed them under the bed because they reminded her of her marriage. She was literally sleeping on her failure, and each time she remembered that they were there, she became upset. When I worked with her, I encouraged her to go through the photographs, and pull out the ones that reminded her of happy times, and to burn the duplicates, the blurry ones, the ones with people she couldn't remember, and the ones that made her sad. I encouraged her to make a memory board and put lots of the happy photographs on there. The others that she wanted to keep she put in an album where she could look at them when she wanted. By doing this, Patricia was able to make a positive connection with her past. Also, she found that by going through the photographs, alone, over the period of a few days, allowed her to express some of the emotion that she had bottled up when she got divorced. She found the process very cathartic, and she discovered that when she looked at the memory board it made her feel more secure in herself and ready to face the future.

Insecurity

When I went through this process, I realised that I had hundreds of books, some of which I had owned since I was a child. Periodically I went through them and cleared some of them out, but it was only when I moved house that I realised what the books had become to me. I had arranged my books so that 'the intellectual ones' could be seen by everyone who came in the house, and the pulp fiction was tucked away in the bedroom, just as I had in my last home, and the one before. The books had become my way of showing how intelligent I was! I realised that this was purely a habit, and I didn't need to have the books on display to show other people that I was well read. I have seen this with clients who have ostentatious displays of the right sort of coffee-table book – supposedly so other people could see that they had taste!

Identity

Some people collect objects. Teapots, anything with pigs on, postcards … Collecting can be a wonderful hobby. For some people, however, it can become a way of giving themselves an identity that they otherwise do not relate to. If you no longer get any pleasure from that collection, or no longer actively participate in the hobby, it can become a burden. When the collection becomes something which just gathers dust, or takes up room in the spare bedroom, it is time to think about getting rid of it, and making room for something new – even another collection, but make it something that you are going to get pleasure from! When you recognise that you are no longer the same person who did the collecting, it is time to move on. Have a good clear-out, and let someone who *does* enjoy those objects get pleasure from them.

It will become clear to you that when you feel secure in yourself, as you will by the time you have completed this programme, all the things you surrounded yourself with that were *purely for show* will go. If you genuinely like and enjoy these objects, you will keep some of them – but their meaning as a reflection of you will be gone as you will feel confident to be yourself, and true to yourself as well.

ACTION
Every day, clear out one small thing. It may be your bedside drawer, it may be your handbag, it may be one shelf in your office. Only do one thing. No more than that. You will start to get into the habit of clearing out, and as you do you will find things that you didn't know you had and either be able to use them properly or discard them. As you clear the space around you, you are clearing space in your mind to become successful. You don't have to become neat – as you clear, your mind will start to feel calmer and more ordered.

Letting go of friends and moving on from people who are no longer of value to you will be covered in a separate section, 'Complainers and sustainers'.

Competition

A lot of manuals and self-help books on success talk about competition, and how you can use it to motivate you. In my many years of practice I have found that competing can be a really destructive force unless you are clear about who you are competing against, and how that competition will affect your motivation.

In *Happiness: Lessons from a New Science*, author Richard Layard talks about the economics of happiness. He states that in the 1950s, we were, as a nation, happier than we are now. We earned less, had fewer choices, less freedom of expression and scope for improvement. Yet we were happier. Why? One of the answers to this puzzle relates to competition. In the 1950s we compared ourselves to our family and immediate social group, and the similarities were stronger than the differences. Now we read about Posh and Becks, we live in a 'global village' and compare ourselves to the rest of the world. You would think that would help us realise how fortunate we are, wouldn't you? In actual fact there is a clear pattern in the media. Rich is equated with happy, and poor with sad. As long as there are magazines that sell because of these images, there will be high levels of discontent.

Why does the media feed this? Simple. If you feel discontented, and you pick up a magazine with a photograph of someone who looks happy while carrying a Prada handbag or the keys to a Ferrari, you will subliminally associate that object with happiness. And you think you can't be hypnotised!

The problem comes when you start buying the products recommended to you, and find that they only make you feel happy for a short while, or not at all. That is when rampant consumerism kicks in as you keep buying to chase the elusive happiness which you were sold in the magazines. This competition is destructive, and only keeps us in the bind of shopaholism. It's time to stop being a victim of the media and start choosing your life. It is incredible how liberating this is, and it doesn't mean that you can't have nice things in your life, but you will recognise that they in themselves do not *make* you happy. *You* make *you* happy.

The only competition which will work in real, practical ways is for you to be competing against yourself. You know your limitations, you know what you are really good at, you know when you can put in more effort, and you know when you are enjoying what you are doing. The only person worth competing against is *you*. Saying that, it is a good gauge when you have a peer group to judge yourself against. These people may be friends, or people that you work with. You can use their reactions to judge how well you are doing. You will lose some of these people along the way as you change and improve, because they won't be able to deal with your change *because it shows them that they could have done better if only they put their minds to it.* You can, and you will be able to, compete with yourself in a healthy and appropriate manner by the end of the programme. There are many suggestions in the CD tracks which will help you to do this, so at this point you do not need to do anything at all, just recognise that **the only person you are competing against is yourself**.

Chapter 3

Developing strength

Chapter 2 walked you through your fears and concerns, and showed you what you have done in the past to stop yourself from setting goals. This chapter will guide you through all the useful things you may already have in place, and how to refine and improve them, so that when you do set the goal (in Chapter 4), you will be well prepared, willing to aim high and able to start imagining yourself as a success.

Confidence

Having confidence in yourself and what you are doing is really important. Sometimes we set out to do things, but even if we have the right idea and techniques to make it happen, if our confidence is low we might decide that we don't really deserve the benefits of the changes. The end result of this is that we fail to dream – to look to the stars.

We end up convincing ourselves that we really don't want anything in particular, and bumble through life pushed and pulled around by whatever life brings along.

With confidence you will start to dream – to recognise that you deserve better, and in doing so you will allow your unconscious mind to work on deciding what you really want out of your life. Confidence in yourself can be quite difficult to define, but you can recognise it through your actions. When you are confident you are prepared to do things, and to take the consequences of your actions. You will not always be right, and this is where I would like to start in helping you define your confidence so you will know it when you have it.

A confident person is prepared:

To be wrong

You are unlikely to get things absolutely right the first time. Making mistakes is all part of learning, and the only way you will learn how you are going to improve is by making those mistakes. Sometimes, making mistakes will lead you to doing things very differently. The importance is that the confident person does not beat themselves up if they are wrong. They learn from it. Enjoy your mistakes – they make you stronger.

To give first

When we are confident in ourselves and in our place in the world, we are prepared to be the one who gives first. If you have had an argument with someone, instead of deciding that, because you are right, they should contact you first – be the strong one and make the call. If you are in business you will learn to give more than the client expects, and that way you will always get referrals and repeat business. If you want someone to be a good friend or contact, be prepared to give your time or information first. It will reap excellent rewards and your confidence in yourself will grow hugely, even if you do not get anything directly from that encounter, **you are learning confident behaviours**.

To ask for help

Those who lack confidence can view asking for help as a sign of weakness. It is quite the opposite. Asking for help is a sign of strength. It shows that you are comfortable in accepting that someone else has something that you want, and that you are prepared to ask for it. When you are confident you will recognise that you can ask for help from many different people, and if they say no to your request, you will not take it as a personal attack. You will find that when you ask for help and receive it you will also be helping other people grow in their own confidence. **Learn to delegate** – that way you will get much more done, and you will be able to achieve things outside of your abilities. I will give you an example: I wanted a website. I had a choice – either learn how to do it myself and spend time and effort doing something which might end up being average at best, or get someone else to create it. I did the latter.

Concentrating on what you can do well, and letting others do what they do well means your rate and capacity for change increases dramatically. If you can't aford to pay someone, do a swap of some kind – or enlist friends and family. People who care about you will enjoy being asked for their help – believe me on this one!

To take calculated risks

You will not always know exactly what options to take up. You might decide to ask other people's opinions, and try to evaluate your decision based on this. Be aware that if you spend too long thinking about relative merits and weighing up the pros and cons of each decision, one of two things will happen: either the window of opportunity will close, or you will suffer from mental paralysis. When you are confident, if you are not sure what to do, you will trust your judgement and make a decision. Taking a calculated risk shows that you can **rely on your own judgement**.

To walk away

Having the confidence to walk away from a project, a relationship, a safety net will often be the hardest thing that you can do. You may find yourself thinking how much time and effort you put into it, but for whatever reason it hasn't worked. You may even try to make it work by using a different technique. Confidence allows you to be dispassionate and lets you know when to draw a line under something and walk away from it. When you have gone through this programme a couple of times and the process has become habitual to you, you will be able to recognise much more quickly when something isn't working – and let it go. When you do, you **clear space in your mind for something which will work**.

To prioritise appropriately

In any project there will always be a number of things to do. When you are confident you will be able to recognise which order to do things in. When you are confident you will be able to spend time making lists and creating schedules which in themselves do not seem to move you any closer to your goal. But you will know that preparation is key to change. When you are confident you will be prepared to stick to your priorities, no matter what else changes. You will also have the confidence to recognise when to put your goal-setting process on hold because something much more important and urgent has come up in your life. When you prioritise and have confidence in yourself you will be then able to get back on course after dealing with the interruption, and you will know in yourself that you are doing the right thing.

Confident people:

■ go with the flow
■ trust their instinct
■ always look forward

If you always look back to the way things were, and not at how they can be in future, your confidence will suffer. By looking forward to the things you will have, you stay excited and therefore motivated in what you are doing now. The confident person is also flexible in their approach to doing things, and will feel comfortable changing their plans as new opportunities arise.

The overriding framework above all of these is that a confident person is *prepared*. If you prepare as much as you possibly can, you are less likely to be taken by surprise when things do not go exactly according to plan. Being prepared also means that if this does happen, instead of thinking that it is a problem, you look for the opportunity within that situation.

EXAMPLE

Mike and Steve were both made redundant at the same time. Both were bored in their jobs and had thought about leaving before. When the redundancies were announced, Mike panicked, and worried about how he was going to pay the mortgage. He saw the problems which could come up now he had been forced to leave. Steve (who had a mortgage to pay too) saw the redundancy as a perfect time to retrain as a driving instructor, something he had thought about doing for a while. He viewed the >>

> *redundancy as a perfect opportunity to do what he wanted to do. The only difference between the two was that Mike lacked confidence, while Steve had it.*

When you are confident, you will look for, and find, the opportunities that are around you. And guess what? People like people who are confident!

Developing a winner's mind

When I decided that I was going to change the life I had for the one that I wanted, the first thing that surprised me was the fact that I didn't really know what I wanted, only what I didn't want. I found that the more I focused on the possible problems I might come across if I *did* do something to change my life, the less able I was to imagine myself successful. What I needed to do, and you can do too, is create a new version of me – a successful one.

I had, by then, read all the books I could find on the subject, I could quote any number of different theories on how and why success strategies can work, and had helped hundreds of people achieve their health, sporting and career goals. Ironic, really, but it is not all that uncommon to be brilliant in theory, but not in practice. To this day I still find it strange to discover any number of coaches, counsellors and therapists who are superb at helping other people, but are not successful themselves, and seem unable to help themselves (or in some cases even to recognise that they have a problem). I realised then that it was only when I was successful in my own right that I could honestly help other people to achieve their goal. Would you want to go to a part-time coach to help you in your career success, or an overweight therapist for weight control? It doesn't make sense, does it? If you want to seek success, then seek the successful.

Once I had made the decision to use the hypnotic techniques – which I had used on others – on myself, I had a new problem. I knew myself, and what I was capable of talking myself out of. So the first thing I had to do was work on myself and my value as a person even before I could get started, and this is the process you will experience next in the programme before you start on your goal-setting. If you don't feel confident, or focused, or motivated, it doesn't matter how good the success strategy is, it will fail because you will not believe the suggestions you are making to yourself! You need to believe in yourself and your capabilities first, before starting to make changes which will be effective for life.

A winner believes, feels and acts like a person who is focused, motivated and confident. I certainly did not have these characteristics when I first made my decision to become successful. Outwardly I may have looked as if I had them, but it was an act. My way of finding these characteristics in me was to study winners and how they did things. I looked for people whom I felt had these characteristics – they were to become my inspiration, my muses. Their voices were the ones I imagined encouraging me when I needed a push. I began to take them around with me like a set of characters in a play. I know, it sounds a little odd – but it worked for me. I thought of all the people I admired and, because I wanted their praise, I kept on pushing myself. I read their autobiographies, learned about their lives – and what I discovered is that they all have something in common, and that is a belief that anything is possible if you really put your mind to it. Thomas Edison said, 'If we all did the things we are capable of doing, we would literally astound ourselves.' He was, and still is, right. Think about it now. When you are very old, do you want to regret what you did – or what you didn't do?

When I started to learn about what success really means, I realised that, although I studied people whom I admired (this is called modelling in neurolinguistic programming terminology*) and recognised the similarities in their psychology, I quickly became aware that we are

---

* Neurolinguistic programming (NLP) is the study of how neurological responses (mental connections), language structures (both spoken and body language) and observable patterns of behaviour are influenced by one another. NLP is not just a commentary, but its exponents also believe that it can be used for an individual to predict the future behaviour and also influence the behaviour of another individual or group. It is used in a wide range of fields from therapy to sales.

influenced by any number of people, some of whom you might *not* admire. When your confidence is low, you are more vunerable to these negative people and opinions. I needed to protect myself, as you will, from those people whose opinions I did not admire. Even when you don't tell anyone what you are doing, people often feel the need to offer an opinion (usually unasked for). It can sometimes be awkward to disengage yourself from conversations of this kind once you are in them. What you *can* do is shield yourself from them. My way is a simple one: I did not (and do not) take advice from anyone that I don't admire. If someone offers me an unasked-for opinion, and I do not admire them as a person, I listen politely, and mentally hit the DELETE FILE button. Listen to people who have achieved something in their lives – if they have not, then remember that their opinion is probably not worth listening to. It will only confuse and discourage you.

To start my journey, before I could trust myself and while I was working on my confidence, I needed a new inner voice. One that wasn't me to begin with, but would help me to become confident and trust my own opinions. The inner voices I heard at first belonged to my muses, then after a while, as I grew in confidence, the voice was just mine. This was when I knew that I had learned to trust myself and my own judgement – that I was confident. You will go through this process too. When you set out on this journey, be prepared to ask people you admire for their advice. You will find that people who are truly successful in their own right are happy to encourage you. You will then find that as you become successful in what you do, and secure yourself, you too will be happy to pass on that knowledge rather than keep it to yourself. I have seen this during my many years of experience in private hypnotherapy practice. I have lost count of the number of clients who then went on to study hypnosis so they could do for other people what my sessions had done for them!

ACTION
Write down the names of three people you feel have one or more of the following characteristics: focus, motivation or confidence. These can be people from your personal life, from public life, or from fiction. Make sure they are people you like and admire! These people will become your guiding voices, your muses, until you find your own positive inner voice.

EXAMPLE

FOCUS	*J. K. Rowling*	*Alan Sugar*
MOTIVATION	*Ellen MacArthur*	*David Beckham*
CONFIDENCE	*Richard Branson*	*Madonna*

While you are *becoming amazing*, these voices will help you until you **find your own inner strength**. If you find yourself in a difficult situation, or with a question and no answer, ask yourself what your muses would do – and go with that. You will find that they push you a lot harder and further that you would yourself, and if you admire them, you will want the qualities that they have too – and you will be brave. You will start to unconsciously model their behaviour as you notice your new ways of thinking start to work better for you than the way you were before. You will model their thought processes, their responses to situations, and very soon – in fact, sooner than you think – the inner voice will be your voice, strong and encouraging. You will have learned to trust yourself.

This ability to listen to your positive inner voice will stay with you as you grow and develop, and it will be your own inner guide, coaching and encouraging you from now on.

No compromises

All the way through this book I will encourage you to change the way you think, act and feel. In this section I want to highlight a very different topic: the areas of no compromise, things that you are not prepared to sacrifice to get your goal. You need to be absolutely clear about what these things are that you are not prepared to give up, or bargain with yourself about. If you start making compromises, and you lose the things most precious to you in your attempts to be successful, then reaching your goal will be absolutely worthless. So, I want to walk you through each area individually, and make it easy for you to put them into the back of your mind where you won't have to worry about them again. Part of the uniqueness about the 'Be Amazing' programme is that it helps you pull out from your unconscious all the really basic things that you should be doing; it checks that you are doing them safely and properly, and then drops them into the back of your mind where they can run like background processes on a computer.

Health

Make no mistake on this one, your health is absolutely irreplaceable. If you sacrifice your health to achieve your goal, it doesn't matter how much fame, praise or wealth you have – it becomes worthless.

Absolutely nothing is worth sacrificing your health for. That also means making sure you do all the right things to safeguard it.

Eat properly

Even if your goal is to lose weight you should eat good, nutritious food. If you are not really all that interested in food, look on it as fuel. You would not expect the engine of your car to perform well if you put the wrong fuel into it, or only a very little – so don't expect your body and mind to perform well if you are doing this to yourself.

The easiest way to get round this, while you are doing the programme, is to work out a weekly rotation of meals, and then make a shopping list of what you have to buy. I know this seems obvious, but once you have done this it serves two purposes. First, it means that you don't have to think about what you are going to eat, so you are not going to forget and skip meals (ending up with low blood-sugar levels), and second, with one less thing to distract you, you can focus on the habits of success which are moving you towards your goal.

ACTION
Write down the following:

MONDAY	breakfast	snack	lunch	snack	dinner
TUESDAY	breakfast	snack	lunch	snack	dinner
WEDNESDAY	breakfast	snack	lunch	snack	dinner
THURSDAY	breakfast	snack	lunch	snack	dinner
FRIDAY	breakfast	snack	lunch	snack	dinner
SATURDAY	breakfast	snack	lunch	snack	dinner
SUNDAY	breakfast	snack	lunch	snack	dinner

Write down your meal plan in each of these sections, and then do a shopping list. You do one shopping trip per week, and then you can forget about food. Remember – this is the fuel for your journey to success.

Brain foods

Unfortunately there is no one type of food that will automatically change the brain chemistry to make you cleverer. However, if you eat food that helps to protect the brain and brain function, then over a period of time you are helping to keep your brain in good shape, sharpening memory function and development of new neural pathways.

Fish is perfect for feeding your brain as it contains protein and a healthy mix of minerals and vitamins, including trace elements, all of which improve brain function. It is also rich in omega-3 which is an EFA (essential fatty acid), one you can only get from your food. Salmon, herring, tuna, sardines, anchovies and mackerel are rich in this oil. If you're a vegetarian, flaxseed oil is a good source of omega-3.

Food rich in vitamin B, folic acid, magnesium, potassium and calcium will also help strengthen your brain and nervous system. I have listed the main food types and their benefit below.

Vitamin B1 (thiamine) – essential for healthy brain and nerve cells. Eat wholegrain and enriched-grain products like bread, rice, pasta, and fortified cereals, and pork.

Vitamin B5 (pantothenic acid) – forms a coenzyme which helps in transmission of nerve impulses. Eat lean meat, poultry, fish, wholegrain cereals, legumes, milk, vegetables and fruit.

Vitamin B6 (pyridoxine) – helps convert tryptophan into serotonin, a brain chemical. Eat chicken, fish, pork, liver and kidney, as well as wholegrain cereals, nuts and legumes.

Vitamin B12 (cyanocobalamin) – helps maintain healthy nervous tissue. Eat eggs, meat, fish, poultry, milk and dairy products.

Folic acid – essential for metabolism of long-chain fatty acids in the brain. Eat bananas, orange juice, fortified cereals, lemons, strawberries, melons, leafy vegetables, dried beans and peas.

The following minerals also play an important role in nerve function:

Magnesium – found in wholegrains, legumes, nuts and green vegetables.

Potassium – found in apricots, avocados, bananas, cantaloupe and honeydew melons, grapefruit, kiwis, oranges, prunes, strawberries, potatoes, meat and fish.

Calcium – found in milk and milk products such as cheese, yogurt, calcium-fortified foods and fish with edible bones.

What you will quickly realise on reading through these lists is, quite simply, to feed your brain you need to eat a healthy, balanced diet, with plenty of fresh foods. You see – it's not rocket science! You know this already, but most people don't turn that knowledge into action.

You also already know that too much caffeine and alcohol are no good for you. I will, as usual, make suggestions in the hypnosis CD tracks so that this knowledge is taken on board unconsciously and you will then feel free to act on it without thinking about it. **You will start to eat healthy, nutritious foods and notice the benefits.**

Drink water

Hydrate your brain for goodness' sake! Carry a bottle with you constantly – without fail. Brain tissue is 85% water and if you don't keep hydrated your energy levels go right down, and you can get headaches and even become depressed. **Drink a glass of water half an hour before you eat, and whenever you take a break from what you are doing.** You will think more clearly, feel more energised and look better for it!

Take exercise

Get off your backside and have a ten-minute walk every day. Don't think about it, just do it. Believe me, this is a brilliant energy and mood boost and it will help you think. You already know that you should be taking thirty to forty-five minutes' exercise of sufficient intensity to raise your heart rate three times per week to stay fit and healthy. Do something you enjoy – sex, dance to your favourite cheesy album, go for a swim. Your energy levels will go right up, you will **feel stronger, think clearer and be more energetic**. What a bonus!

ACTION

Schedule exercise into your diary – this is an appointment with your health. No compromise. Ten minutes per day for walking. A forty-five-minute blast three times a week.

Did you know that if you take a forty-five-minute walk, four times a week it can help you lose around eighteen pounds in a year!

Core values

The significance of good health is the same for everyone. There are, however, other areas that need to be acknowledged, and considered. These are unique to each of us, and are known as core values.

A core value is any area of your life that you define as being of such importance to you that you are not prepared to compromise on it. Recognise what your personal core values are and you will be taking the first step to making sure that you don't accidentally cross one of your own boundaries. This is very important and will help you when personalising all aspects of this programme so it will remain workable for you as your life changes and develops. When you have done the action described below, you will find that it has an impact on the next section of the 'Be Amazing' programme. If you fail to do this properly, you might find that you do not move forward with the programme because you are unknowingly harming one of your core values.

EXAMPLES
My religious beliefs and observations
Time spent with my family
My relationship with my partner

These core values become your boundaries. Know your boundaries – and stick to them. As you change and develop when you *become amazing* it is important that you remain *you*. If you get your goal, but your behaviour and personality change for the worse as you work for it, then the goal is worthless. It becomes a hollow victory. People who stay true to themselves and their friends and family are the real winners.

List the areas of your life that you are not prepared to compromise on, including your health and fitness as well as your core values.

When you have written these things down, you will have a way of reminding yourself what is important to you. Put it in a place where you can see it every day. Keep reminding yourself of what is important to you and you will always stay on track.

Get this part right, and everything else will start to fall easily into place. By the end of the next chapter you will have created the right kind of mental image and you will have the confidence to go for it. When you know what you really want, how to get it and how to get started will become much clearer too, as the unconscious part of your mind will start working these other elements out for you **without you even trying**.

Now it is time to listen to the first hypnosis track on the CD. This is the 'Confidence' track, and you can do this as often as you like while you are doing the programme, but make sure that it is on a day when you are not listening to any of the other tracks. It is important that you give your mind time to absorb one set of suggestions without confusion.

ACTION

Go to the toilet if you need to.

Turn off your phone.

Choose a time and find a place where you can be undisturbed. You can sit down, or lie down, as long as you are comfortable. Do not cross your arms or legs – allow them to relax.

If you wear glasses, take them off.

Now listen to the 'Confidence' track on the CD.

When the track is over, sit or lie still for a few moments to make sure you are fully reorientated.

Remember: if anything happens that needs your attention while you are listening to the CD, you will become fully alert and able to respond. Afterwards you can continue where you left off.

Chapter 4
Know what you want

OK it is time to get on with it. Accept it – the only time to get started is now. You have had false starts before, so this is it – no more excuses, no more tricks, no more postponing. You didn't pick this book up because you are content with your life – no one does. Keep reminding yourself of this. You are reading it because you want more. You picked up the book because, for whatever reason, the idea of a transformed life appeals to you right now. So, no more unrealistic promises to yourself – now is the time to start. Easy to say, isn't it? Here lies the root of one of the most annoying pitfalls – and a lot of people fall into it. It is called the postponement trap. This is the situation: you decide to get started; then a little unconscious voice starts planning excuses – that you will start it next week, or next month, or even next year. This voice is about to get a new tune to sing, one which will get you moving, and I will do this through the hypnosis CD tracks. By now I bet all you want to know is how to get started. It is easier than you think – by picking up this book **the process of changing your mind and your life has already begun.**

What you really, really want

In Chapter 1 I walked you through what it means to *be amazing* and how it is going to happen. In Chapters 2 and 3 we went through the obstacles and ways of increasing your confidence in yourself. This chapter is where you start work on the programme itself. By the end of the chapter you will have worked out exactly what it is you want out of the process. This is a vital step in *becoming an amazing person* – first you have to work out what it means to you to be a success. Not in vague or woolly ways, like 'being happy', or 'getting a better job', but in a clear and specific way so there will be no more confusion. Without confusion, you will be able to work on getting what you want out of life *unconsciously*. Also in this chapter I will use the second hypnosis track, 'Amazing You', to 'fix' the suggestion into the unconscious part of your mind.

If you don't **know what you want** yet, that's fine. Later on this will fall into place for you. There will be actions for you to do which will help you work things out properly. Remember, not all of the actions will apply to you, so if something doesn't ring bells, that's fine. You will only work through what is relevant to you.

At this point you will be starting to **unconsciously decide** what you want out of this programme. What is important for you to know is that there is no **need to**

think hard about it. At this point a lot of your ideas will be unconscious. Let this thought drift to the back of your mind for now, where your unconscious mind can work on it.

This is the chapter in which I will tell you all you need to create your own, personalised goal, and use the second hypnosis CD track to fix it in place. The new goal you are going to create here will show you how your life is going to be when **you are amazing**. Why do you need a new goal? I will tell you why. If the goal you already set was good enough before, you would already have achieved it. The big differences this time are that by the end of the chapter you will have a workable, personalised goal, and also, because you now understand why you failed before, you won't be able to trick yourself with the same mistakes again. This is important – because once you recognise that the problem wasn't you, but the way you put the goal together, then **your confidence will grow** and it will then make success into a habit rather than a one-off event.

OK, so how do I find out what I really want?

Deciding what you really want is a big step. It will involve you forgetting about what you *think* will solve your problems, and recognising that what you *feel* is important in your life. There is another part to this, and that is knowing the difference between what you want to happen, and what you believe it will do for you.

I will cover the first point in a later chapter. The second, that of attaching meaning and feeling to your goal, and why it is a problem, I will cover now. Below are a couple of examples of what I mean.

EXAMPLES

I want to be slim, because when I am slim I am happy with myself.

Or:

I wish I had a better job, because if I had a better job I would be more confident.

In the two examples there is a goal – being slim – and an effect – being happy with yourself. The big problem with linking a goal and an effect is that one does not necessarily follow the other, and when you get your goal you might not get the effect you expected. The net result is that after everything you have done to achieve your goal, you end up undoing all your hard work. This is because the feelings you expected to have did not come automatically once you had got your goal. This is classic in the case of the yo-yo dieter. They lose weight because they believe that they will feel better when they do, and everything will be all right when they are slimmer. When they lose the weight and the feelings do not automatically follow, they become depressed and comfort eat – repeating the same pattern time after time.

This time, you will set your goal in realistic and recognisable terms – not emotions. This time you will know when you have got what you want – *and the feelings you want to have will follow.*

So how do I get this right?

To get this right you need to decide, in clear and obvious terms, who, what, where, when and how it is going to be for you when you have got what you want – when you have this new life that you are aiming for. To do this there will be a few short and easy exercises to do so you can personalise the programme and set your first goal. Then I will ask you to listen to the second of the hypnosis tracks. This track will 'fix' the positive suggestions into the unconscious part of your mind where they will start making the mental connections you need to work towards your goal – and achieve it.

Through using the programme in one-on-one sessions, I have noticed that most people fall into one of these traps:

- only knowing what you don't want
- wanting too many things
- wanting things over which you have no control
- wanting an emotion, not an end result

In the next sections I break down these traps so you will be able to **work out exactly what you want**.

I'm not sure what I want

This is a really common problem. Sometimes we have to start with what we don't want, and work backwards. Other times there are hidden reasons holding people back from becoming successful.

Habit

Anyone can fall into the trap of easy habits.

Failing to dream and set goals can become a habit. If you can't remember the last time you set out to achieve something and got it, then you are out of the habit and need to relearn it. It is incredible how easily we can get into habits which seem to take us further and further away from our dreams of the life we want. We get into routines of getting up, going to work, coming home, watching TV – and life just ticks by. In fact, the longer there is between deciding to do something and actually getting on with it, the more difficult it seems to become. How often have you set out with a new year resolution only to turn round and it is already March and you haven't got started yet? It's time to get back into the habit of dreaming and aspiring.

Habits are easily broken – *if you have something better to put in its place*. Some of the suggestions on the CD will help you to find better habits. Using the hypnosis to do this can work better than trying to work it through by using written exercises. This is because habits *are* unconscious. The hypnosis suggestions will work directly with your unconscious mind – to erase the habits that keep you from achieving your goal, and install habits that will help you to get what you want. You are going to learn that **success is a habit**, and one which, once you start setting goals as a matter of course, becomes unconscious and – best of all – easy.

Ignorance

We often have no idea what we are capable of doing when we put our mind to it.

Please understand that when I talk about ignorance I do not mean that you are ignorant. Far from it! What I mean is that there is an ignorance of what is possible, of what is out there for you. Successful people are ignorant too, but their ignorance is different – they do not know what is *impossible*. This works in a strange way for them. If you don't know what you can't do, and you try and succeed, you get into the habit of doing things differently from other people. So, stop listening to other people when they tell you it can't be done. It is better to regret what you have done than regret what you haven't done!

How?

The first thing you need to work out is:

What do you want – specifically?

This is often the hardest bit to get right. We usually know what we do *not* want. We do *not* want to smoke. We do *not* want to continue in this relationship. We do *not* want to be fat… The list is endless. Herein lies the irony – by banging on about what we do *not* want, we build a really strong memory of it into our brain, and this strong image is often what stops us from making changes in our life.

EXAMPLE
Do not think of a white horse, and then do not think of a red monkey in a waistcoat riding on that horse's back – make sure that you are not thinking about it, in fact think of something completely different instead.

What happened? The harder you tried to *not* think about the image, the harder it became to get it out of your mind. Where am I going with this? Well, to get what you want you need a new image in your brain – a positive one which will motivate you and take you forward. So instead of deciding on what you *don't* want, it's time to work out what you *do*, so that your brain can create the image, and you can start to make it real.

I want too many things

We all want different things, sometimes lots of things. Some people, when they come to see me to *become amazing* find that when the idea of changing their lives with hypnosis becomes a reality, they suddenly have a shopping list of all the things that they want in life. Wanting too many things all at once is a trick that our unconscious mind plays on us to stop us from changing anything. When we want too many different things we become overwhelmed, like a kid in a toyshop who wants it all. The end result of wanting too many things is stress, and this stress stops you from being able to make decisions – so you end up achieving none of your goals and becoming more and more frustrated.

> **EXAMPLE**
> *I want to lose weight and get a new job and change my relationship and learn how to speak French...*

All of these are perfectly good goals, but if you want them all at once and try to work on them all at the same time, you will get overwhelmed and either fail to start, or do them in a haphazard way and not achieve any of them properly. If you are someone who has lots of goals, list them down.

ACTION

Get a pad and pen and take ten minutes to write down your goals as a list. Do it now. Spend ten minutes on this at most. Don't worry about whether you think they are useful goals or not, just write them down. There is no need to put them in any particular order.

Now you have listed out your goals, I want you to look for the simplest and easiest goal to achieve. Not the most important, or the one that you feel will change your life most, but the easiest to achieve. This is the first goal you will work on.

Have a look at the examples at the end of the book if you need some inspiration. In there you will find examples of goals, as well as success habits and starting-off points (the latter two you will come on to later in the programme).

Why?

When you work on the easiest goal first you create a new neural pathway quickly and easily. If you have already succeeded in the past you may be using a path which was already there. The repetition in the programme reinforces these new pathways in your brain as you keep going over the same ground, and makes them stronger and more easily accessible. These pathways are designed to be used time and time again. The pathways become templates for success which nothing will be able to overwrite.

You have done something similar before. It is exactly the same as when you learned to swim or drive, or learned any activity that then went on to become unconscious. You start with the simple and easy, and progress once it has become automatic and you don't have to think about it any more. You don't start out on a busy road or in heavy traffic when you're learning to drive, do you? Of course not. You start where it is quiet, and where you can concentrate on what you have to learn to move the car around. It's only when driving becomes a habit that you are safe to go out where it is busy and deal with all the other things that can happen when you are driving. By going for the easiest goal first you are easing yourself into a new way of thinking. One which you will then use to get all the other goals on your list! You will also be able to recognise any pitfalls or tricks that may have been preventing you from succeeding before. So, by concentrating on the easiest goal first you are clearing the path for all your future successes. When you do it this way, you quickly *become amazing*. Almost without noticing, **you become more confident and successful each time you set and achieve a goal**. By doing the easiest first, your confidence in your ability to do the next easiest, then the next will grow as you think less and less about what you are doing, and more and more about what you are going to get out of doing things differently.

I want things I have no control over

Sometimes we want things which we know in our heart of hearts are unrealistic, or at best very improbable.

> **EXAMPLE**
> *I want to win the lottery.*
> *I want X to fall in love with me.*

When we daydream of things which are unlikely to happen, this too is a trick that our unconscious mind plays on us to keep us in the holding pattern of our daily lives. Our unconscious mind is a funny creature, almost a mind of its own – and it doesn't like change. It also doesn't communicate too well with the logical and conscious part of our mind either. In fact, these two parts of the mind only really communicate fully in sleep, when we dream – or when we are in hypnosis. So, when your unconscious concentrates on daydreaming of the unrealistic, it is a way of distracting you away from the things that you can achieve – will achieve. Once you make the decision to let go of impractical daydreams you free up your mind to become a winner – and most importantly to take control of your own destiny.

Some of my clients get stuck on this one, and say, for example: 'Well, someone has to win the lottery.' When they talk like this, I respond with: 'Yes, it happens to some very lucky people – but until then, I will teach you the tools to change your life for yourself.' There are other people who think that successful people are 'lucky' – somehow in the right place at the right time and with the right idea.

Henry Ford, who created the first production-line motor car, had a great response when people told him he was lucky when he did what he did. Ford said: 'The harder I work, the luckier I get.' I'm with Henry Ford on this one. It is true, there is such a thing as luck – but it is something you create yourself. When you start acting on the suggestions in this programme, you will find that other, positive things which you had not thought about start to happen.

For example, you might need someone or something to help you with a particular aspect of your goal. When you started you had not got a clear idea about how this was going to happen. Then when you started thinking and acting like a successful person, suddenly what you needed to progress came to you. It is often in a different form to the one you had expected, but this will happen to you – time and time again. I know this from personal experience. It has everything to do with how you sense the world around you when you are focused on achieving something. You start to see things around you that you hadn't noticed before – hear snippets on the radio that are relevant, have conversations with people who know someone who can help you. You can call it synchronicity if you like, or karma, or give it any spiritual meaning you wish to give to it. Me, I am a very practical person. I prefer to think that all the things that suddenly seemed to appear which helped me towards my goal were already around me, waiting for me to notice them. You will notice this too as it happens to you.

There is a final factor to this section. When you recognise that what you were wishing for is simply not going to happen by chance, you free up that part of your thought processes to get to work on making real changes. Let it go – it is as simple as that. Make the decision to free up your mind to change your life and stop allowing the unconscious part of you to block the change. When the unrealistic image of what you wanted is gone, there is space for what you can and will change. The successful individual *knows* that letting things go, no matter how much time, effort or emotion we have put into the project, is one of the keys to success.

Amazing you

To really know what you want, you need to create a mental picture of your life as it will be when you have achieved your goal. This is most easily done by imagining trying to describe to someone else what is happening in a photograph – one with you in the picture. The image you describe must mean only one thing – must not be open to confusion or interpretation. Stay away from vague words such as 'very' or 'little' or 'more', because they mean different things to different people. Think of creating this image as a game – one which you will win when your description cannot be misunderstood or misinterpreted. For example, saying your goal is 'a new car' is too vague for this process. To use this process to get your goal you need to describe 'a 2007 Mitsubishi Evo in white'. This way your brain has something really clear to fix on – and you will work towards that!

You need to describe this picture in terms of how it will look, sound, feel, even smell and taste.

If you really have *no* idea of what you want, you will know what you do *not* want. You can then start the thought process off by putting down what you don't want, and then flipping the coin over. Sometimes what you discover will be a bit of a revelation.

EXAMPLE

I don't want to work for someone else any more.
Turn the sentence over and you find:
I want to work for myself.

When you start this process you stimulate a very different part of your brain from the usual parts which would be involved in thinking. This allows you to think about different ways of doing things. Using the hypnosis part of the programme you will involve the part of the brain involved in anticipation and preparation. What you are going to do when you create this image is very similar to what happens if I ask you what would you like to eat for your next meal. You start to imagine what you would like. When you do this, you stimulate your digestive system, and your stomach starts to rumble and your mouth to salivate. This is a conditioned response – where our internal system can respond to something that is not actually present. When you make the successful image of yourself – the one in which you have achieved your goal – you create a similar state of unconscious anticipation. This will become the engine that will drive you towards your goal.

It is now time to A.M.A.Z.E. To create your goal, you are going to use the following criteria. I will give you examples which will help you be really clear on getting this right.

The goal needs to be:

Attainable. This means it has to be possible for you to achieve it with what you have already. If you want to run a marathon in a week, you need to have that level of fitness in place, or you won't get it.

Measurable. This means that you can quantify the results in concrete terms – so that anyone looking at the goal would be able to understand what it is, and so will know when it has happened.

Accurate. Make the image as specific and precise as possible – so there is no room for confusion. Use some form of measurement in your description. Make it so you could describe it to anyone and they would understand.

Zoned. Zoned stands for time zone. Timing is everything. Have a fixed date in mind for completion.

Exact. To get the image clear in your mind, use as many of your senses as possible to create it – what it will look like, sound like and so forth.

EXAMPLES

Examples of goals that won't AMAZE anybody:

Money
To have enough money to be comfortable　　*Not exact enough*

Weight
To be thin enough　　*Inaccurate*

Career success
*To build up a multimillion-dollar enterprise
in two weeks*　　*Wrong time zone*

Relationships
*To be happily married to (put any film star's
name here)*　　*Unattainable*

Health
To get fit in two days　　*Unmeasurable*

EXAMPLES

Examples of goals that will AMAZE:

Money

Driving a brand new Lexus SUV in silver with blue leather interior and smelling the scent of new car when I drive away from the showroom

Weight

To fit into my interview suit by March and notice the looks I am getting

Career success

To have a personal assistant by next May and hear her voice answering my calls

Relationships

To live with my partner by January and feel his arms around me when I wake up

Health

To run a half-marathon by June next year and feel the competitor's medal round my neck

You can see from these examples how to **get it right**. Anyone reading these goals would understand what they mean. These goals are not abstract concepts, but can be seen, heard or felt by anyone. With a goal set like these you will know when you have achieved them – so there is no room for you to trick or convince yourself otherwise.

ACTION

Take fifteen minutes at most and write down your goal. When you have done this, use the AMAZE. criteria to challenge it. Ask yourself the question, is it Attainable Measurable Accurate Zoned Exact. Keep going back to the list above to check against it. If it doesn't fit all of the criteria, change it until it does. Use the examples above to guide you as well. By the end of the fifteen minutes, you should have a simple sentence that fits AMAZE.

Now you have clearly defined your goal, it is time to use the hypnosis to 'fix' it into your mind, where your unconscious can start to work on making it real.

It is time to listen to the 'Amazing You' track. The purpose of this track is to take all the elements of your goal, and put it firmly in the back of your mind. Once it is there it will stay there. You will find that as the days go by, you will think of your goal more and more, and it will progressively start to become more real to you – without you having to do anything consciously at all.

ACTION

Read through your goal.

Go to the toilet if you need to.

Turn off your phone.

Find a time and a place where you can be undisturbed. You can sit down, or lie down, as long as you are comfortable. Do not cross your arms or legs, allow them to relax.

If you wear glasses, take them off.

Now listen to the CD track, 'Amazing You'.

When the track is over, sit or lie still for a few moments to make sure you are fully reorientated.

Note: It is a good idea to have a drink of water after the hypnosis, as you may feel a little light-headed. This is *not* a side effect of the hypnosis, but happens because most of us forget to drink enough water, and when we are focusing internally (such as in hypnosis), we become more aware of our body.

Now you have 'fixed' the first part of *becoming amazing* into your unconscious mind. That's enough for today. Do something else. Pick the book up tomorrow. You need to get at least one night's sleep to begin to let this sink in properly. Also – don't talk about what you have just done, with anyone. You can discuss it with anyone you like soon enough – but only after a night of sleep. I will explain the neurology of why I have asked you to do this later in the programme. The nice thing is, if you are not interested in why, you can skip over that bit when you come to it.

For now – rest. **You will sleep well tonight**.

How to Get
What You
Want

Chapter 5
Mind games

The first section of this three-step programme has now been completed. Easy, wasn't it? Your goal is safely in place, and now fixed firmly in the back of your mind where you can forget about it for now. This section will be even easier than the last because you will recognise the steps as you go through them, although this time the content will be different. In this chapter I will walk you through the minefield that is your mind. You can be your own worst enemy – I think you already know this. By the end of this chapter you will understand the mind games you have played on yourself in the past, so you will **never be able to trick or fool yourself ever again**.

What exactly is a mind game?

A mind game in the context of this programme is a set of unconscious mental programmes, sometimes known as schemas, which are set off in response to a specific situation. For example, there you are, walking down the street one day, feeling pretty good about yourself until you meet an old friend who tells you how well they have done since you saw them last. You walk away from the encounter feeling irritated and discontented, and thinking 'lucky devil'. Why? I will tell you. The encounter triggered a schema – a preset pattern – in your brain that predetermined your reaction. Rationally, you thought you were really pleased for him to have done so well, but unconsciously you felt resentful because *you knew you could have done at least as well if you had only put in more effort*.

Mind games then, fulfil two functions:

- They are the unconscious mind's way of prodding you when you have failed to live up to your own expectations.
- They allow you to fool yourself into thinking that you don't need to take an active part in your life for things to happen.

Mind games are so destructive. The worst part about them is that they are habitual responses. Most of the time we are not even aware of them.

EXAMPLE

Christopher had always done what was expected of him. He had worked hard at school, taken the job in the bank, got a mortgage, got married and become a parent. He was not, however, happy. When I worked with him we looked at his belief systems, and the >>

---

major mind game he recognised was based around the idea that if he did everything properly (his term, not mine), then he would 'obviously be happy'. His mind was setting him up with a schema that said 'Do it all by the book and you will reap the rewards.'

When Christopher worked through the 'Be Amazing' programme he recognised this mind game, made himself consciously aware when he was doing things just 'because they were the right thing to do', and started to do things which made him happy, even though they weren't 'by the book'. The framework of 'Be Amazing' made it safe and productive for him, and he and his family became much more relaxed and happy as a result.

Recognising your own mind games can be virtually impossible, unless you have a partner you trust and feel comfortable asking what tricks you play on yourself. Even this can be problematic, as we rarely like to hear from someone else that we are capable of fooling ourselves. So, forget about this for now. You can leave this to the hypnosis CD tracks. I have made suggestions there which will help you do the following:

- recognise if you are tricking yourself
- stop before you act on it
- do something different and more helpful instead

You will, for a while, be more aware of your behaviour, and, once the suggestions start to take effect, you will **leave these tricks in the past – forget about them, they are not your problem any more**.

Believe in yourself

There is another great quote of Henry Ford's that I often use to remind clients how much their attitude about themselves alters the world around them. He said: 'If you believe that you can do a thing, or if you believe that you cannot, in either case you are right.' This is so very true. When it comes to believing in yourself this is the bottom line. When you start believing in yourself, 'Be Amazing' starts to become the most natural thing in the world.

Whether we believe in ourselves depends on many things, most of which cannot be seen, touched or heard – they are feelings. To anyone else around, these are intangible, but to the person experiencing them these feelings can be the thickest, tallest wall in the world lying between themselves and their future success. They may feel that they will never get beyond this wall. You will break down this wall, and use the rubble to build steps for your future.

Our beliefs about ourselves have three main contributing factors:

- how we grew up
- what is around us now
- our dreams of the future

Past – helpful and harmful memories

Let's start with our history. Fact: we cannot change what happened or didn't happen to us in the past, but what we can change is how we *respond* in the here and now. This is about choice and control. Once you feel you have options, then you can make choices. If you feel you can make a decision about those choices, then you have control. If you do not believe in yourself, then how can you make choices, how do you get control? The answer is that you don't, and even if you do, the changes you make in your life will be short-lived, just like the woman who leaves her husband, only to return repeatedly, even though he mistreats her.

As before, I have worked into the hypnotic suggestions on the CD lots of self-belief. These suggestions are designed to help you to **feel more positive and confident, more focused and motivated**. Above all, these suggestions are designed to help you to **recognise the choices you can already make, and take back control of your life.**

All of the suggestions on the CD which relate to self-belief will be taken on board unconsciously, so you will not

be immediately aware that you are feeling better about yourself. In addition, you will, by the end of this programme, feel **you can make a conscious decision to be a success**. Then, instead of revisiting the negatives that brought your self-belief down, you will **allow yourself to go back into your past and pick out the memories you want to motivate you**.

EXAMPLE

Julia was bullied at school. As an adult she lacked confidence. Once she realised that her poor confidence stemmed from what happened to her at school, she made a conscious decision to beat the bullies – to become a winner. From that point, every time she went into a situation where she used to feel a lack in confidence, she remembered the bullies, and said to herself, 'You won't beat me – I am the winner here,' and she soon started to feel as confident as she had always wanted to be.

So, first of all, know your enemy. What is it from your history that has held you back?

ACTION
Read the action through first, then do it.
Take ten minutes and sit down or lie down – close
your eyes and concentrate on your breathing.   >>

Slowly count down from ten to one, using your out-breath to time the counting. When you reach one, let your mind wander and allow yourself to remember a time when you did not feel confident. Think of who was around you, remember as much about this situation as you can. Allow yourself to do this, and give the time a name (e.g. the time when I was UNHAPPY, ASHAMED, SAD, BULLIED). Once you have it, give yourself the suggestion that IN FUTURE, IF EVER I THINK OF (the name you gave to the time you remembered), I WILL USE IT TO SPUR ME ON, TO PUSH ME FORWARD. I AM WORTH MORE, I WILL WIN, I BELIEVE IN MYSELF.

Shout this in your own head as loud as you can, fill your mind with these words, and take as long as you like to do this.

Then, slowly count up from one to ten, using your in-breath as a guide. Gently open your eyes and read on.

Now write down the phrase that you shouted to yourself:

IN FUTURE, IF EVER I THINK OF…I WILL USE IT TO SPUR ME ON, TO PUSH ME FORWARD. I AM WORTH MORE, I WILL WIN, I BELIEVE IN MYSELF.

If there is something in your history that still affects your self-belief, you should be able to remember it in that exercise. If nothing comes to mind, then it is not because there isn't anything to remember, but that there isn't anything *relevant* to the way you are feeling now. If the latter is the case, your attitudes from the past will not hold you back from completing the programme.

History can drive us forward, or hold us back. It is your choice.

The action below is one you can do regardless of whether you found something in your past or not. I want you to think of something you have achieved in the past and how good it made you feel. This action will help you switch that good feeling on in future, whenever you need it to motivate you.

ACTION

Read the action through first, then do it.

Take ten minutes and sit down or lie down – close your eyes and concentrate on your breathing.

Slowly count down from ten to one, using your out-breath to time the counting. When you reach one, let your mind wander and allow yourself to remember a time when you felt confident. Think of who was around you, remember as much about this   >>

situation as you can. Allow yourself to do this, and, when you can really remember this vividly:

GENTLY SQUEEZE THE TIP OF YOUR THUMB AND FIRST FINGER TOGETHER, TO MAKE AN 'O'. RELEASE THEM AS THE FEELING PASSES.

Then, slowly count up from one to ten, using your in-breath as a guide. Gently open your eyes and read on.

From now on, when you go to bed at night, after something positive has happened to you during the day, you can repeat the exercise above, and 'fix' that positive feeling into the movement of your fingers. Whenever you want to experience that positive feeling, you will squeeze your fingertip and thumb together again, and the feeling will come back to you.

Present – what else will change in your life when you succeed?

When you change, the world around you changes too. You notice different things, and other people become aware of the differences in you. Once you become more confident, you will notice things that you aren't happy with. They were there before you noticed them, but now you are confident you become more able to think about doing something to change the situation. The change in the way you think about things will cause your behaviour to alter as well. There will be a ripple through everything you have contact with as you start to develop. This is natural. No change occurs in a vacuum, and you need to accept that not all of the effects of your change are predictable. When you change, your world changes – and for some people this creates fear. If a person is insecure, and unassertive, then the familiar is preferable to taking action – no matter how bad their present situation may be. This is why, when you make changes in your life, you have to own that change and take responsibility for it. Otherwise you will sink back into old patterns, not because they are better, but because they are familiar and 'safe'.

EXAMPLE

Marianna noticed when working through the 'Be Amazing' programme that she was having more arguments at work, and her partner did not seem to be very supportive when she discussed these problems with him. As we continued to work together, Marianna became aware that as her confidence grew, and she started to show signs of developing, some people around her viewed this as detrimental to them. They preferred her as she was. Marianna realised one of the hardest lessons of change: when you change, >>

---

there will be knock-on effects that you have not considered. She decided that her current work situation was one in which she could no longer develop, and she left. Not long after she also left her partner – as she recognised that he was not developing with her, and that her development would be stifled if she stayed. Even though she loved her partner, she realised that her love for him was not sufficient to keep the relationship going, as the person he loved no longer existed.

The change that you make is like dropping a pebble in a still pond, the ripple goes much further than you think – you will find yourself growing and developing much more than you could have believed. When you *become amazing*, you don't just become a little bit amazing – you have the potential to be much more than even you know. Allow yourself the freedom to let your ideas about your life fly in front of you – and when you start to really trust your instincts you will not only *become amazing*, but will be amazed at how far you came.

Let it go – it's not worth it

Too often people spend time and energy getting upset, annoyed and angry about things that other people have said and done. The successful person does not. He or she has learned that expending pointless emotion and effort over a situation that they cannot change – for example, someone else's feelings – is a waste of energy. This is where you might be accused of becoming hard and uncaring since you started this process, because you recognise your boundaries and stay safely within them. I will give you an example. In the past, when someone you cared about got upset because you did not remember to call them at a certain time, you may have got upset yourself. Now you know what your boundaries are, you can stay calm and explain to them why you did not call at that time – without getting upset yourself. Strong boundaries are important as they will protect you and help you assess whether you are responding appropriately or not.

If you have an argument, as does happen in life, take a step back. Consider whether you or the person you are arguing with is tired or stressed. Do not automatically assume that their reaction is anything to do with you. You are not responsible for other people's reactions, and there will be situations where you do not get the response you expected. If this is the case, let it go. Move on. It is a waste of time and energy to try to second-guess *why* another person reacts in a specific way. If you have a close relationship with that person, you can ask them, 'Are you OK, because you would not usually get so upset?' But remember that men and women are different in how they respond. Men generally respond better to action, women to discussion. However, this is not about the difference in how men and women react to situations, it is about how you deal with something which, in the past, you would have chewed over.

To make this simpler, allow yourself a period of time to be irritated, or hurt. I usually make a cup of tea and sit quietly. As long as I am drinking the tea I let myself analyse what happened, and my reaction to it. I don't let anything else interrupt me. When the tea is drunk, I move on. If the situation was particularly unpleasant, I will occasionally allow myself a few minutes throughout that day to go back to it – but once I have gone to bed that night I will **never feel that negative response again**. You see, during our REM sleep we process the events of the day, so if this problem is one you have had, allow the suggestions on the hypnosis CD to **put those old negative responses to bed, once and for all**. You will be prompted throughout the book when to listen to the tracks, so there is no need to do anything at the moment.

Once you get into a routine of allowing yourself a short time to focus on something that has upset you, and then making a conscious decision to let it go, your unconscious mind will learn from these encounters, and you will stop assuming that you are to blame for the event, or that you are responsible for someone else's reactions. Let me make this crystal clear. You are only responsible for your own reactions – no one else's. That is not to say that you would ever treat someone else without respect – but the choice each individual makes about how they react to the world is theirs alone. You will find that when you have completed the programme and understand yourself and your own failings better, you will be more able to understand whether other people are reacting appropriately or not. You will be more tolerant of other people and their problems – but you will no longer allow them to affect you in an inappropriate way.

There are other encounters in life, especially when you are changing, that can sometimes seem like a setback. When you are working towards your goal, and you are making progress, if something happens which sets you back, or something doesn't happen that you wanted to happen, it can feel like failure.

EXAMPLE

Paul wanted a new job. He went for an interview for his 'perfect job'. He didn't get it, and felt very down as a result. I worked with Paul using the programme to help him recognise that it was only one job of many that he could do and would enjoy. We worked on his confidence and Paul started applying for other, better-paid jobs – ones which he knew that he would enjoy. He got three offers in the first week of applying.

Sometimes you need to take a step back and recognise that if something does not happen the way you wanted it to, there may be a very good reason for it. In fact, there may be a much better opportunity round the corner. Move on – keep focusing on your goal, and you will start to see these minor hiccups as interesting interludes instead of problems.

When you make a conscious decision to get up, get over it and move on, you find that this becomes a habit. A much better habit than brooding and looking back. Keep looking forward – that is where your success lies. The successful person recognises that things will not always happen the way that they expect them to happen. So, instead of seeing a setback, see it as a challenge. Successful people view all of these events as challenges, puzzles, things to work out rather than be disappointed by.

As I worked through the programme myself, and found myself heading up what felt like dead ends, I soon started to realise that the *way* I got to my objective didn't matter, provided I stayed true to myself and kept my objective clear in my mind. In fact, I discovered that if I kept my options open about *how* I was going to achieve something, my unconscious mind would come up with a much better solution than the one I had originally thought of. This is a classic example of thinking too hard about something! It is the same when you try to remember someone's name – and the harder you try, the more you seem to forget. Later on, when you're not trying, the name pops into your head. Start to trust your unconscious mind to come up with your answers. As usual, if any of these patterns are a problem for you, there are suggestions in the 'Be Amazing' CD tracks which will help you.

Be honest about what you want and your ideas. If you don't want to do something, say so. If you do want to do something, say so. Life becomes much easier, more fun and much more exciting when you stop trying to live up to somebody else's expectations of how your life should be run, and what you should be achieving. By deciding on a goal, and working honestly towards it, you will make the life you live into the one you want – not someone else's dream, but yours.

In all fairness to the people around you it is vital that you keep communicating your intentions to those whose lives will be affected. You do not have to tell everyone everything, but keep them informed of what is happening in relation to how it will impact on their lives. If you don't, those people will become afraid of the changes in you, and may try to sabotage them – even those who genuinely care about you – because they get afraid of what those changes mean. I mentioned this earlier in the example of the husband whose wife lost weight and he became afraid of losing her as a result. If you find that you don't want to tell someone what you are doing, ask yourself why this is. If it is because you know from experience how they will react, and you are afraid of that reaction, you need to ask yourself whether this relationship is a healthy one for you. Change is the best way of testing a relationship. If the relationship is not strong enough to sustain change, then the foundations of that relationship are not stable. You may find that as you get more confident, and more in control of what you are doing in life – especially when you start to see the benefits – other people around you may change in an unpleasant way. Sometimes, the effect of *becoming amazing* is that you will have to change your environment, and the change in your life will reach further than you initially imagined. Accept it – you can live the dream, but you have to dare to dream it first.

EXAMPLE

Adam worked in an office and was constantly having ideas. When his ideas worked, his colleagues would be unpleasant and scathing about them, saying, 'I could have done that if I wanted to.' His boss didn't give him the support he needed because he didn't want to rock the boat or seem to show any favouritism. Eventually, Adam left the job and set up his own company, where he started to put his ideas into action. With no boss but himself, and by surrounding himself with positive, enthusiastic people, his ideas quickly made him a millionaire – and a happy one at that.

This is all very well for you to say, but what if things don't work out the way I expect them to?

In the past my clients would sometimes come to me frustrated when their strategies for change didn't work out according to the way they planned it. I will say to you what I say to them. Accept it. This is real life. If we try to map out every step of the journey we are bound for failure. The thing to do here is to make sure that you don't see variation in your route as a setback. It isn't – it is a deviation, and one which will often end up being a better route than you originally planned.

If you don't get what you want, work out the benefits of not having got it. 'The job wasn't for me', 'That relationship didn't really suit me.' When you *become amazing* you will find that you constantly (and unconsciously) keep revising how you do things. When you do this you will start to welcome the distractions rather than fearing them.

Future – what are you afraid of?

There is a curious phenomenon which I have observed through my years of practice. When it comes right down to it, and people really think about what they want out of life, more of them are afraid of what will happen when they succeed than if they fail!

There is a quote from Mark Twain on this topic. He said: 'I have known many troubles in my life, and most of them never happened.' This is a perfect description of how we can get locked on to predicting disaster – and a great excuse to do nothing as a result.

EXAMPLE

Greta hated the life that she had. She felt trapped, stressed and insecure. When she thought about the ways in which she could change her situation, she realised that she constantly talked herself out of her options. When we worked together, I pointed out that she was suffering from 'yes, but' syndrome. Every time she came up with an option for change, she followed it up with 'yes, but …' and talked herself out of it. Greta's problem was a lack of self-confidence which meant that she always looked on the black side – seeing problems rather than solutions. When Greta's confidence started to grow, she began to work out the benefits of change, rather than focusing on possible problems. This was difficult at first, but as she started to see the results, her confidence developed and she began to try out different things without predicting disaster as she had before.

The only 'but' in this programme is the one you need to kick!

Fear and excitement are physically identical, did you know that? When you get into either of these states, your sympathetic nervous system kicks in, producing adrenalin and your senses become heightened. The potential problem is that when we are stressed we can sometimes mix up the reactions, and learn to fear the very things we should be enjoying. We need adrenalin to kick-start change, and dopamine to feel good when we are involved in the activities that stimulate us. Deep in the brain there is an area called the nucleus accumbens, more commonly called the 'reward centre'. It works by responding to a cascade of neurotransmitters, which in turn release dopamine into the brain to make you feel good. If what you are doing does not make you feel excited enough, you will not stimulate the brain in this way, and you will very quickly lose your motivation. There will be no thrill.

When you set your goal, it has to excite you – get your pulse racing, stimulate you to action. If it doesn't already, change it until it does – make it bigger and brighter – more exciting so that you really start to want this goal with a hunger and passion. Then, when you think about your goal, you will start to get excited at the thought of it. In the past you may have interpreted these physical reactions as fear – but from now on you will recognise that this is excitement, and an essential ingredient in getting what you want out of life. Who wants to be dull and boring? Set your pulse racing. Put a little zest into your life – it's time to live not a little, but a lot!

Before you get too hung up on how you are going to do these things, all of the suggestions in this programme, both on the pages and on the CD, are designed to help you reprogramme your brain to get precisely what you want out of life – without any conscious effort at all. You will only notice or pay attention to these suggestions when you feel they are relevant to you, and you will only act upon those that are safe and appropriate for you to act upon. I want to reassure you at this point: it is you who will be reprogramming your mind – not me. *You* will be taking control of your life, not someone else. This programme is all about you taking and keeping control of your life to allow you to make the decisions that you want – safely and easily. All you have to do to make this happen is to work your way through the programme, and the changes you want will already be happening for you.

For now, just read, listen to all the CD tracks when instructed, and work through the actions if they are relevant to you. There is no need to think about doing anything just yet. **Change, when it is to be long-lasting, will happen naturally and effortlessly**, and it will happen for you this way, this time, and from now on.

Chapter 6
Motivation

Motivation can be a big issue for some people. Often when clients come to me and I explain to them that hypnosis cannot make you do anything that you couldn't do already, nor can it put something into your mind that wasn't there before, they can be disappointed. I point out to them that I wouldn't like someone making suggestions to me that I hadn't had time to think through. Nor would I like it if someone suggested to me they could *make me* do things – as if they are in control, not me.

Hypnosis is all about control – putting the control of your life squarely back where it should be: with you. Hypnosis will teach you how to control your thoughts and ideas, and, when necessary, change them for ones which will work better for you in future. Hypnosis also, and most importantly here, acts as an amplifier. It can and will only amplify the positives – because of the way the brain creates images it cannot accept negative suggestions when they are made in hypnosis. You know that in the past, either consciously or unconsciously, you have made suggestions to yourself about what you are going to do in the future, and how you are going to feel. You pre-plan by suggestion. What the hypnosis does is takes this natural process and turns it into a mind boost – one which will motivate you not just today, but for the rest of your life.

If it's so simple, why can't I motivate myself?

Ironic, isn't it? There is one voice that we consistently ignore, and that is our own inner voice. This happens especially if we are demotivated or feeling insecure. We are not inclined to listen to ourselves when we make suggestions especially if we have talked ourselves out of things in the past.

EXAMPLE

You decide that you are going to go to the gym every morning. You even get all your kit ready the night before so that you will be able to get straight out of the house. Then one day, you sleep through the alarm and don't have time to go to the gym that morning. The next day when you wake, do you get up and go to the gym? No – you lie in bed thinking, 'One more day off won't matter – I had a heavy day at work yesterday and I could do with the rest.' The next day and the next it gets progressively more difficult to get out of bed and to the gym – and a month later the gym bag is still sitting there by the front door, accusingly.

We are really good at convincing ourselves that staying the same is preferable to changing.

Why is that? It is quite simple really. If we have to think about doing something, we will analyse it, and weigh up the pros and cons of action. If we are demotivated we will pick inaction and, to make it more palatable, we explain to ourselves why that was the right option. We can be so convincing that we will genuinely believe that doing nothing was the right option to choose.

So how do I break this pattern?

Doing nothing to change your life is a habit – nothing more. You have probably got so used to talking yourself out of doing things to change your life that you are not even aware that you are doing it. In other words *it has become unconscious*. So, here is your problem and your solution. To break the pattern you need to alter the way that you unconsciously think, feel and act – and to get properly motivated it needs to become unconscious. When your motivation is unconscious – in other words when you are not thinking about what you are doing any more, you are just getting on with it – *you can no longer talk yourself out of action!* When this happens – and it takes around three weeks for any change to be taken completely on board – you will **be motivated**. And, most important of all, instead of thinking about what you are doing – you **just do it**. When you just get on with things you start to find that it creates less stress and takes less effort than avoiding doing it. In fact, some clients have told me that once they **get motivated and just do it** they have more time because they used to spend longer avoiding doing something than the time it took to actually do it.

The significant difference here is when you start to see the benefits of your activities, this in turn will feed your motivation. You will find yourself responding to the appropriate suggestions from the 'Motivation' track on the CD if you need a boost here.

Go for a walk – get those neurons firing

Walking is a success secret. Make a ritual of it. Go for a ten-minute walk every single day. So, what is the big deal about walking? I have already talked about how important walking is for you in terms of your physical well-being and health. There is another secret to walking, which is even more significant than the physical benefits, and that is *walking is a workout for your mind*.

There are two aspects to this. The first is that when you get out and walk you are exposing yourself to sunlight. This then stimulates the pineal gland which produces chemicals called tryptamines. These chemicals enhance your mood and you will automatically feel more cheerful, **and think more positively about life**.

The second, very important fact which will motivate you to get out there and walk is this. At the Sisters of Notre Dame convent, 668 nuns have been participating in a long research project on Alzheimer's disease. This project, headed by David Snowdon, PhD, of the University of Kentucky, has been looking at many different aspects of the nuns' lifestyles and how these affect tendencies to develop Alzheimer's. He has discovered, among other factors, that those nuns who took regular walks were considerably *less* likely to go on to develop symptoms of the disease in later life. His theory is that by walking you are stimulating the peripheral nervous system and firing off a bio-feedback process which then feeds back to the brain itself. You are giving your brain a workout!

Protect your brain – take it for a walk daily.

ACTION

Create a mood board or notebook. Put inspiring photographs or pictures on it, along with quotations that inspire you. Put images on it that mean something in relation to your goal. You can always look at it if you are flagging.

Musical interlude

I also take time out to listen to music which will stimulate me mentally. It has been shown by research that listening to Mozart stimulates mental connections. Frances Rauscher, who did the original research in this area, called it the 'Mozart effect' and discovered that playing Mozart to both adults and children increases their spatio-temporal reasoning – in other words it helps them to **think more efficiently**. In the experiment, listening to Mozart's Piano Sonata in D major raised spatial reasoning test scores. The effects were significant, but short-lived.

Now, whether you like Mozart or not is a different matter, but in the short term it helps you to think differently by stimulating brain networks through other pathways than those you usually use. By stimulating your brain in unusual ways you are going to make alternative neurological connections which would not otherwise have been made. Use the time when you are listening to the music to reinforce your goal by daydreaming of your future, when you have achieved your goal.

Research has also proved that listening to music reduces stress levels, so that will be a bonus, as when your stress levels are lowered, you think more clearly and more effectively.

Some Mozart suggestions:

Piano Sonata in D major (K488)

Finale: Molto allegro, V, from Sinfonie in D, 'The Peasant's Wedding'

Theme with Variations from Serenade No. 10 in B major 'Gran Partita' (K361)

Romance and Adagio from Serenade No. 10 in B Major 'Gran Partita' (K361)

Andante, II, from Serenade No. 3 in D major (K185)

Andante grazioso, V, from Serenade No. 3 in D major (K185)

Andante, II, from Serenade No. 4 in D major (K203)

Adagio, III, from Divertimento in D major (K205)

ACTION

Sit down or lie down and listen to one Mozart piece. Concentrate on your breathing and focus on allowing yourself to breathe deeply and well, letting your body relax on each out-breath. Count down from ten to one, using your out-breath as a guide when you count. Take yourself forward in time and imagine yourself living your dream, watching the world with the eyes of someone who has already achieved that goal, feeling the world around you and hearing its sound.

Bring yourself back to the present by counting up from one to ten, counting up on your in-breath, becoming progressively more energised as you do.

After doing this you will feel motivated and stimulated. Each time you take yourself into this state of concentrated attention you are creating and reinforcing mental connections that take you progressively closer to your goal. You are making the image of your success state a stronger image each time you do this. The result will be that **your confidence will really start to rise**.

Later on, in a section called 'Theme-tune your life', I will talk about how to use different types of music to motivate you.

Be the one others envy

Have you ever wondered why some people are successful?

You probably know someone who always seems to be achieving something, having ideas, getting excited by life. You might think that it is easy for them, and come up with any number of reasons why they are successful. You might even be a bit envious. You now have a choice: spend the rest of your life being jealous of other people's success, or go and get some of your own. It is time to become the one other people envy. When you think like a winner, your whole world is different, not just your attitude. You think about what is going on around you and, instead of looking for problems, you look for solutions.

Success is all about attitude, and when you get that right, everything else falls into place. I often find, when I work with people one-on-one, that they keep surprising themselves when synchronicity starts to happen. The thing is, there is really no such thing – all those opportunities that suddenly seemed to appear *are already there*. They already exist, and – let me tell you this right now – if you don't see them, someone else will.

Success is a state of mind, and it starts with competition. Not in competing with other people, because there will nearly always be someone richer, more famous, faster than you. True competition starts with two things:

First, recognise that the only person you are competing against is yourself. At one time, we would only compare ourselves with our friends and family, and a small social group around us. Because of TV and the Internet we compare ourselves with a much wider group. Now we are comparing our lives with those of Posh and Becks. No wonder we get discontented with what we have.

Second, realise that you can do more if you put in the effort. Successful people go looking for success, dream success, smell, taste and touch success. With 'You Can Be Amazing' you can too.

'You Can Be Amazing' teaches you how to recognise the chances that are already around you, and how to make more. It shows you that you do not need more of anything to start becoming successful – you don't need more time or more money to get started on becoming a success. You first need to recognise what you have, and then decide how to make it work for you.

When I first put this programme together I recognised something – that I had been putting time and effort into envying other people and their success, and making up reasons why it was obviously so easy for them. More time in fact than I spent on my own success. Having done this, I was then justifying why it was *not* so easy for me, and giving myself permission (and a clear, direct suggestion) to fail if I tried. So I didn't try. It is far easier to do nothing, then there is no danger of failing – it's obvious when you think about it! The envy acted as a barrier to my success. It is incredible how easy it is to fall into this trap – you may have done so in the past yourself – and once you are in there it is simpler to decide to do nothing. You can decide that how you are and what you are doing isn't that bad, really.

The problem with this attitude is that it takes us away from looking at ourselves. If we spend time envying other people, and deciding that success came easy for them, we are missing a massive point. Successful people don't envy other people's success – they applaud it. Once you are a winner yourself you recognise the effort that went into any achievement – and you stop wasting time and energy envying other people. Envy is a real enemy of success. So what is there to do about it?

How do you feel about those things now, when you are the person being envied?

One of two feelings will appear. You will recognise that the envy is either unfair or pointless:

- There are some things out of your control – like your height
- There are other things that you have to work to achieve, like a nice car

So you let go of the pointless envy and concentrate on what you can change.

Instead of envying others, it is time to have other people envy you.

What I want you to notice at this point is that, if you want, you can use envy to your advantage. If you know what it is that you want out of the programme already, you can write down what you want other people to envy you for, once you have achieved your goal.

People will envy me my ...

Examples: wealth, strength, freedom, attitude, style, relationship.

Now write down how you are going to feel when this has happened.

Now I have achieved this, I feel ...

Examples: fantastic, inspired to do more, pleased with myself, ready for anything!

Envy from other people will happen quickly when they start to hear, see and feel that you are moving forward towards your goals. Recognise their envy as a sign that you are making progress!

Positive images

Fill your space!

Confidence has a form – and that form is the way you choose to hold your body. If you carry yourself well, you will give the impression that you are confident. This posture becomes what is known in NLP terms as an 'anchor'. An anchor is a trigger that sets off a chain reaction of emotions, thoughts and responses – and in this case the reaction is to feel confident. You are literally getting into shape for success. When you stand taller you also breathe better, and you look slimmer and healthier. People will respond to you differently when you create that first visual image that tells them you are a confident person. You have twenty seconds to create that first impression – use it well!

It is also worth being aware of the fact that when you make new and unfamiliar movements, especially if they are exaggerated at first, research shows that you are stimulating proteins which create new neural pathways. This is the same way that children learn when they copy what they see in front of them. They are creating the pathways that become essential to unconscious learning. When you change your posture to an unfamiliar one, and copy the successful shapes of other people, you are creating a mental mindset of success – unconsciously.

ACTION

Go out for a walk, or find a bench or a café in a busy outdoor location where you can sit and watch other people as they walk. You will quickly notice who looks confident and who doesn't. You will find they all have characteristics in common – walking tall, head up, face forward, unhurried, shoulders down and arms relaxed.   >>

Next, get up and practise a confident walk, a posture, a way of carrying yourself. When you go out in future, take your walk for a test drive. This will feel odd at first – but tell yourself AS SOON AS I WALK OUT OF MY FRONT DOOR, I WILL WALK THE WALK OF THE CONFIDENT. Very quickly it will become automatic.

Theme-tune your life

Like a character in a movie, I have a theme tune. In fact, I have a number of them, depending on what I am doing. I have put these on my iPod, and when I need a boost, I crank up the volume. If I need a lift in an emergency, I play these songs in my head. It gives you such a buzz, and is a brilliant way of changing your state of mind.

EXAMPLES

MOTIVATION *Who Are You? – The Who*

FOCUS *The Duet from* The Pearl Fishers *– Bizet*

CONFIDENCE *Sisters Are Doin' It For Themselves – Aretha Franklin*

Take ten minutes and list some tunes under the headings of MOTIVATION, FOCUS and CONFIDENCE. Make sure they are uptempo, the words are positive, and they make you smile!

Whenever you need these moods, the songs will be there in your head, waiting to play.

Eye contact

Confident people look you in the eye. They don't stare, but they do make sure that they make eye contact with the person they are communicating with. It is incredible how many people we meet on a daily basis and we do not even look at them! Could you describe the person who sold you your newspaper today, or your sandwich at lunchtime? I thought not. It's time to start looking people in the eye.

It is a well-known secret, but I am going to tell you it again: When you look people in the eye *you make a connection with them*. People respond incredibly well if you look at them – you open up dialogue. This doesn't work with everyone, obviously, because there are people out there like you used to be, who avoid eye contact. However, more people than you think will respond to you when you make eye contact – and you may even get a smile out of them.

Throw away your scruffy clothes

There is a funny thing about keeping an old baggy pair of trousers for when you are going to paint the garden fence. If they are comfortable then there is a temptation to wear them, just around the house, of course, I mean you wouldn't dream of going out in them. Then one day you run out of milk, and you think, 'I'll just nip down to the corner shop – no one will see me,' and so you do just that – and, surprise, surprise, you see your ex-boyfriend or -girlfriend with their new partner. Bugger! It's too late – you are now convinced that they think that you've gone downhill since you split, and your confidence is somewhere in the seat of those baggy trousers. If something you love is past its sell-by date – junk it. It makes you look past it too.

This doesn't mean that you have to be smartly dressed all the time, but what it does mean is that it is time to update your wardrobe to suit this new, amazing person that you are becoming. Clothes *do* matter. Think about it – would you want to be seen by anyone who is in a position to make a decision about you in your really scruffy clothes? Grungy is fine if that is your style, but show that you have put the effort into your appearance and you are showing self-respect. Show that you respect yourself, and other people will show it back to you.

Complainers and sustainers

The complainers are the people in your life, who, when you have met up with them, make you feel worse than you did before you saw them. Sustainers, on the other hand, will always make you feel better than you did before because they are so positive and encouraging. There is enough material on this subject for a chapter of its own. I am going to talk about these concepts in terms of how they can influence you on your way to *becoming amazing*. Think of your address book and the people in there – your family, friends, work colleagues, people you know casually. There are a lot of them once you start looking at it. All of these people will have some form of claim on you and your time.

If you put your primary relationships at risk, your goal may become an empty one, because you end up with no one to celebrate it with. I use the word *may*, because you might find that it becomes clear to you that the person you are with is not right for you, and you stay with them out of habit. Please remember: when you make a change, even a tiny change in your life, these changes have an effect on the world. As you change you may not even be aware of how it is going to affect the people around you, but it will happen. By communicating with those people who matter to you, you are encouraging them to support you. By not telling them, you can create fear and anxiety in them which can then become destructive. I showed you this in the example I used before about the woman who lost weight and her husband became afraid that she would leave him.

It is important to keep in your mind that as *you* are changing and developing, *they* may not be. They might not understand (or want to understand) why you are doing things differently from the way you did before. Remember: people can be very afraid of change. If this is the case, reassure them of what you are doing, and if they don't like it – tough. If they really care about you, and not just what they get out of their relationship with you, then they will understand and support you.

When I teach hypnotherapy to people who want to learn it as a profession I will always issue a caveat – one which can be scarily accurate. If you go on a therapy course it can be the quickest route to the divorce courts. This is because the person on the course becomes self-aware and changes their behaviour, and their partner doesn't! This can be true when you *become amazing* – some people simply will not like the new you. That is why maintaining your confidence is such a big deal in making this programme work for you in the long term – not just as a one-off. Listen to the 'Confidence' track on the CD whenever you need it – even after you finish the programme. It will help you deal better with the people around you. This is important, to ensure that when you have got your goal other people around you don't pull you down. Remember, you worked hard to get this, and no one has the right to take it away from you, no matter what their reasons.

As you change and develop, other people may need to be given time to get used to the new you. When they see that they have nothing to lose and everything to gain, then they will support you. If they are only in a relationship with you for their own gain, then they are complainers, and are the sort of people you will lose touch with along the way.

Learn to forgive people – genuinely. You can forgive a person even if you find it difficult to forgive what they did. If you don't learn to forgive, you will carry the emotional burden around, and it will become like a weight. If you really are frustrated, beat up a pillow and scream and shout. It is incredibly cathartic.

You can help someone change from complainer to sustainer. You do this by being interested in them, their lives, their needs, and asking them for help (even if you don't specifically need it). Help them to see that by helping you they are *becoming amazing* themselves. Tell them specifically what you want from them by way of help. They will then feel safer and less threatened by your change. They will be more supportive, and can genuinely encourage you as you develop.

This isn't always going to work for you – and in those situations, recognise these people for what they mean to you, and allow yourself to absorb the appropriate suggestions in the 'Confidence' track.

Now I have gone through with you the reasons why you used to talk yourself out of success, and you now have better ways of reacting. From now on **you will feel, look and act more positively**. Get this part right, and everything else will fall easily into place. By the end of the next chapter you will have decided on the success habits and you will add motivation to the confidence that has now taken root in your unconscious. Now you know what you *really* want, how to get it will start to become clear, as well as how to get started, as the unconscious part of your mind will start working out these other elements for you **without you even trying**.

Now it is time to listen to another hypnosis track on the CD. This is the 'Motivation' track, and you can play this as often as you like while you are doing the programme, but make sure that it is on a day when you are not listening to any of the other tracks. It is important that you give your mind time to absorb one set of suggestions without confusion.

ACTION

Go to the toilet if you need to.

Turn off your phone.

Choose a time and find a place where you can be undisturbed. You can sit down, or lie down, as long as you are comfortable. Do not cross your arms or legs, allow them to relax.

If you wear glasses, take them off.

Now listen to the 'Motivation' track on the CD.

When the track is over, sit or lie still for a few moments to make sure you are fully reorientated.

Remember: if anything happens that needs your attention while you are listening to the CD, you will become fully alert and able to respond. Afterwards you can continue where you left off.

Chapter 7

Work out how to get it

Habits of success

Whether you are aware of it or not (and mainly you are not), we all have habits. Some of them are annoying, some of them endearing to our loved ones, some of them are essential to daily life. The habits I want to talk about here fall into one of two categories. Habits that are going to help you, and those that can potentially hold you back from getting what you want out of life.

First of all, what do I mean by habit? In this context I mean a pattern of thought, action or feeling which is spontaneous – something we do not even think about, we just do. A safe habit is one which will move you on the road towards your goal. A dangerous habit is one which will distract you, or even harm you.

To make lasting change happen, you need to understand the importance of turning your new patterns into successful habits. When you have done this, you won't have to think about them any more and, better still, will not be able to trick yourself out of doing things.

A habit is simply a thought or action which we do without conscious awareness, and we have lots of them. Examples include the smoker who lights up a cigarette, without thinking, each time the phone rings, or the person who reaches for the biscuits every time they make a cup of tea. Habits are natural and essential to us. They are designed so that we can respond spontaneously to a critical situation, and can be aware of what is happening around us while still able to function (such as when we drive a car). The only problem with a habit comes about when we want to change one consciously.

Like the man who wanted to give up smoking, and tried really hard NOT to think about a cigarette when he was in the pub. The problem was that the more he tried NOT to think of it, the stronger the unconscious image of smoking became. This is why I use hypnosis in the programme to change the habit on an unconscious level – the level at which it operates. Once you access this area of your mind, you can then install strong, useful habits to replace the negative, useless ones. By installing and refining useful habits in hypnosis, you will be able to carry out the new actions which then take you towards *becoming amazing* effortlessly – unconsciously. Your mind will then be free to think of other things that can take you towards your goal.

I have got lots of habits – how do I know which are going to be useful?

The difference between 'good' and 'bad' habits here is whether they help or hinder you in getting what you want. We have lots of habits which are useful in some situations. Being able to drive a car is a very good habit – but this is a habit which won't help you if you want to improve your fitness levels. A useful habit moves you towards your goal, such as getting your gym bag ready the night before you go to the gym. When it becomes a habit, then it becomes a trigger for going to the gym.

Identifying useful and useless habits is a perfect starting-off point. That way you can eliminate all the things that you won't have to worry about. To make this more clear I will give you an example. You may have a fantastic habit of doing all your filing as you go when you are at work, and that helps you know that you can find your paperwork whenever you need to. It will not help you lose weight if this is your goal. More specifically, useless in this context means that *it will not help you with your goal*. Useful habits will. What is the point in listing them? Well, once you have done this, you will realise just how many habits you have, not all of them useless/bad, some of them useless/good – and you might need them for other goals!

Make a list of the habits you are aware of. Write them down under two headings, USEFUL and USELESS. For the moment it is enough to write them down. In the 'Habits of Success' CD track, I will make hypnotic suggestions to 'refresh' useful habits, and 'replace' useless ones.

If it ain't broke, don't try to fix it

Never try to change *how* you do something if it already works for you. It is a mistake that many people make to try to change the *way* they do things, especially if the way they work suits their personality. This programme is designed to take the elements which you already have in place that work for you. A good example is the student who would like to be able to plan out her essays and do a little work each day – but what she actually finds herself doing is very little for most of the time, then working like crazy for a couple of days before the deadline. If she still gets the grades, why should it matter? Change only the things that *don't* work for you.

What sort of character am I anyway?

It is worth noting the character traits you already have so you can utilise these when working towards *becoming amazing*. Better to do this than to try to change your character – this simply will not work. I have listed some groups below and their characteristics so you can see where you fit in, and recognise which of these will be useful for you.

Steady workers:	You work consistently from start to finish.
Adrenalin junkies:	You know your deadline, and do very little until you are almost on top of it, then you start working.
Slow slow, quick quick slow:	You work hard for a while, then you slow the pace down, but you can pick up again if you need to.

If you are a steady worker, you will find this next section easy because it is all about being consistent and building regular habits, something you already do. If you are an adrenalin junkie, you are going to need to change the way you do things initially, so the habits of success will 'fix'. Once this has happened, and it will take around three weeks, you will start to use your 'deadline dread' again, and get your adrenalin fix, but this time it will be helping you *towards* your goal, not away from it. The final group, which I called 'slow slow, quick quick slow' are halfway to success habits already. This group just needs to vary the habit tempo to a more regular beat until the habits of success are in place.

For now, how these changes will happen is not relevant to you. I will make the suggestions in the hypnosis CD tracks – and you will pick up on the ones which relate to you. I will make all of these varying suggestions to help you to vary your pace in the next CD track. Your character will *not* change, but the way you do things for a little while (the next three weeks) will change – long enough to make the neurological connections needed to set successful habits. These pathways will be used not only for this goal, but in future for all the other goals that you are going to set and achieve. **Success is a habit, and once you start on it, you are well and truly hooked!**

I know what I want, I don't know how to get it

The first part of *becoming amazing* is now in place – you know what you want. The next step is to work out how to get it. But how? First, I want you to be aware that now you have got your goal clear in your mind, unconsciously you will start to come across all the things that you have in place already that will help you. It is the same as what happens if you want a red car – you see them everywhere. Or women who want to get pregnant and see babies everywhere. What is out there hasn't changed – but how you *perceive* it has.

Once you recognise that you already have most of the things you need to create your habits, you will feel much more in control about the whole idea of making these habits part of your life.

ACTION

I would like you to list everything you already have which can be useful for you. List them under two headings:

1. The people around you
2. Skills and equipment you already have

Once you have done this, you will quickly realise that you do not need anything more than you already have to set habits for success. If you think that you need extra equipment or skills, look for the different ways that you already have in your life of achieving the same goal. Instead of dreaming of a personal trainer, look to the people around you to help you achieve a similar result. You may have friends you could persuade to lose weight with you and you can support each other. In terms of the skills and equipment you already have, it could be the park around the corner from the office where you could go for a walk at lunchtime to get in half an hour's exercise, or the exercise DVD that you never opened. Look to what you already have rather than looking outside for your solution.

EXAMPLE

Susan set her goal, and that was to lose two stone by Christmas. Her error was to believe that there was only one way of doing it, and that was to go to the gym. When Susan finally found a gym (which seemed surprisingly difficult) and started to go, she found that she was quickly making excuses to miss her gym sessions. Working through the programme, Susan realised that she hated the gym, and therefore looked for excuses to do anything else rather than go there. I asked her to list all the other ways in which she could exercise without going to the gym – and she came up with a list of physical activities, and people she could do them with. I asked her to identify the one she would most like to do, and the person who she could do it with. Susan started swimming, and encouraged her sister to come along with her. They motivated each other, and had a good time swimming. Susan no longer made excuses as she started to enjoy seeing the improvements. Going swimming became a habit to her – no longer something she could trick herself out of, even if she wanted to, and the weight came off steadily and naturally.

Putting in the effort

Most people will say that they have tried hard in the past to get their goals. Let me now break the reasons for failure into sections, and you can see if you fit into any of these. If you don't, you can skip through this. If you do, there is an exercise for you at the end. Remember, I am only talking about the sort of effort you put into your success, not the effort you put into any other area of your life.

I have always been a hard worker. That was never my problem. My problem was the fact that when I knew I had something important to do, I would make a note to myself that I really needed to get on with that job, I would psyche myself up to do it, and then I would immediately go away and do something else. Clever, huh? I lacked focus, and it was only through admitting to myself that I had a problem, and then using the programme to get the focus I needed, that I finally started getting the jobs done which would help me towards my goal.

People who want something for nothing

If you want a quick fix without any effort, or for someone else to put the effort in for you, this is not going to work out. OK, it's tough-love time. If you don't put in the effort you will not get anything worth having. If you want to spend the rest of your life complaining about how hard done by you are, and that you have been handed a raw deal by life, I have no time for you. Wake up – you are alive, you have choice.

Enough of the sergeant major. If you really want to *be amazing* you have to take control of your attitude. You can and you will have the life that you want if you **put in the effort**, and the only way you will do that is if you recognise what is in it for you to change.

EXAMPLE

Erika came to see me because she wanted to lose weight. She had bought herbal supplements, slimming teas and beauty treatments that promised 'inch loss in minutes'. When I asked her what had worked for her, she admitted that nothing at all had actually worked. I started using hypnotherapy with Erika to help her improve her confidence before we started doing the programme. She admitted that she knew that diet and exercise were the only ways to lose weight, but she didn't think enough about herself as a person to put in the effort needed to lose weight.

With the 'Be Amazing' programme, Erika gained the confidence and self-esteem she needed to get started on an appropriate diet and exercise programme. Once she started seeing the results for herself, her confidence grew even more, as did her enthusiasm.

If you always do what you have always done, you will always get what you always got. In other words, if it hasn't worked before, it is not going to work now. So forget it.

There is no miracle cure for weight loss, but you can make it as effortless as possible by using this programme. Regardless of what your goal might be, you must put in the effort to achieve it. This programme is about changing your long-term attitude towards what you can do with your life, as well as getting your immediate goal.

Believe me, making something look effortless takes a lot of hard work.

People who work hard on the wrong stuff

Then there is another group of people, and these are people who work hard, and are always busy, but seem to get no closer to achieving what they want.

There is an old saying which goes: 'If you want something doing, ask a busy man.' The basis of this is that a busy person knows how to get things done. However, the saying does not mention whether the 'busy man' is happy, or stressed, or fulfilled. The truth is, busy people can be very productive. The main problem with people who work hard but don't get what they want out of life, is that they are *busy doing other things – not things that will take them towards their goal.* In fact, they may feel that they are too busy working and earning a living to have a successful career, or set in motion the brilliant idea they have of setting up an online business. Working hard is important – of course it is. If you don't put in the effort

you will simply not achieve your goals, nor, ironically, will
you enjoy them anywhere near as much as when you do.

EXAMPLE

*Christine works really hard, in fact she is always on the go. She is an
achiever and anyone looking at her would assume that she is a
success because she gets things done. However, she came to see me
because she felt stressed and was sleeping badly. She also felt that
she wasn't making progress in terms of her career goals. When we
looked at the events that filled her day, we quickly found that none
of the things she was doing throughout her working day were
activities which moved her towards her goal. Some of the jobs were
essential, but others she could delegate if she wanted.*

*When Christine reached this stage in the programme, and she
worked out all the activities that did move her towards her goal, she
also realised that she needed to learn how to delegate, and to say 'no'
to taking any more jobs on. The problem here was her confidence.*

*Once she got on with the programme, Christine started to feel
less stressed, more relaxed, and slept better. She could now find
time to schedule the things to move her forward, such as updating
her CV, and registering with some agencies. As soon as she started
to do this, she felt so much better about herself, and it showed – she
got offered a promotion.*

When you set out to become amazing, *remember that it
isn't* how *much effort you put in, it is the* sort *of effort you
put in that makes the difference.*

People who get distracted

The next group are those people who work hard for a bit, then stop, then work hard again. They work sporadically, picking up the work as and when they feel like it.

EXAMPLE

Caroline wanted to start up her own business. She had the idea a couple of years ago, and had been doing bits and pieces towards it in between work and home. There were times when she found a lot of time to work, and others when she felt she had to concentrate on her family or job. By the time Caroline came to see me, someone else had had the same idea, and was very successful at it.

When working with Caroline we quickly realised that she was afraid of how the success of her own business would potentially change her relationship with her partner. Using the 'Be Amazing' programme I helped her to get the confidence she needed to deal with the impact of change on her relationships. Caroline is now working on another business idea, and the programme has given her the focus and determination to make sure that no one else gets the chance to beat her to it!

If you recognise yourself in this description, you will know that each time that you go back to the job you were doing, it gets harder and harder to motivate yourself. It becomes more of a chore, and so you do things less precisely. You make mistakes and have to go back a few steps before you can progress forward.

The worst part about working sporadically towards your goal is not that you have to backtrack all the time, but the fact that you might find your idea overtaken by events. Ideas have a shelf life for all of us, and if we don't get on with them and **put in the effort consistently**, then they can become redundant.

While we are on the subject of working regularly, it is also worth remembering, when you are setting up your success habits, that after forty-five minutes of work, your capacity to perform will shrink rapidly and the law of diminishing returns starts to apply. So practise your success habits in short frequent bursts to maximise the benefits of your efforts.

Little and often; that is the way to succeed when you are working towards your goal.

People who start well...

Then there is the final group of people, those who start out really enthusiastically, they buy all the kit, tell everyone what they are about to do, and as soon as they have done these things they lose enthusiasm, and grind to a halt, like a clock running down.

EXAMPLE

Paul wanted to run a half-marathon. He bought all the right gear, and asked a runner friend to work out a programme for him so he could build up his stamina. For the first couple of weeks, Paul stuck to the programme, but then noticed that there was a book at home on running that he would like to read, so instead of going running that day, he decided to finish the book. The next day he ran, but really felt tired. Progressively he found any number of things in the house to distract him. It became easier and easier to find other activities to do instead of going running. Eventually, as he could no longer complete the programme before the day of the half-marathon, he gave up running altogether.

The next year, he came to see me and we worked together to get his mind in shape for the run. By focusing on his motivation and keeping the appointments with himself he completed the marathon the following year. Most importantly, he didn't use the breaks in his routine as an excuse for failure.

To make this work, you are going to stick to your schedule. You are making appointments with your successful future. It is essential that you keep them.

Success habits are not about a one-off event. These are the repetitive activities that you have to do day after day, week after week, until you have forgotten that you are working towards your goal. When this has happened, nothing can distract or deviate you from your success. These ways of thinking and doing become part of you, and how you operate in the world around you. By the end of the 'Be Amazing' programme, these habits will be firmly 'fixed' into your unconscious mind where nothing and no one can ever disturb them.

When you are working out your success habits, schedule them for the times of day when you are at your best. If you are a lark, do them in the morning, if you are an owl, do them in the evening when you are at your most active. Use what you know about yourself to make these patterns work best for you.

You will refine them, though. At night, when you sleep, when you dream, you will remind yourself of these habits, and constantly seek more effective ways of doing them. That is part of what is so special about the 'Be Amazing' programme – when you have read through the book, listened to all the audio tracks, and carried out the relevant actions, **your way of thinking, acting and feeling will have changed for the better, for ever**. This will all have happened unconsciously, so you didn't need to try too hard, in fact, you didn't need to try at all. You will notice, even now, that you are starting to think differently, even if you are not already acting or feeling differently about yourself. It will come, and sooner than you think.

Now it is time for you to write down the steps that you are going to take towards *becoming amazing*. These are the actions that you will repeat and repeat until they become habits to you. Before I ask you to write down your new habits, I have put down a few good and bad examples.

EXAMPLES

Examples of habits that won't AMAZE anybody:

Money
I will feel better if I save some money regularly.

Weight
I will keep buying exercise DVDs until I find one that will work for me.

Career success
I will keep reading the appointments page of the newspaper until I find my perfect job.

Relationships
I will stay with the man I am with until the one I feel is the one for me turns up.

Health
I will keep reading health magazines until I find a technique that works without effort.

If you apply the AMAZE criteria to the examples above, you will notice that they just don't fit. This is why they won't work. Habits, like the goal itself, must AMAZE. Have a look at the examples of good habits.

EXAMPLES

Examples of habits that will AMAZE:

Money
Every day I will put £1 into the savings jar.

Weight
Every day I will eat a healthy breakfast and will walk for ten minutes at lunchtime.

Career success
Every week I will apply to another agency and phone the agencies I am registered with. I will attend business networks once a month.

Relationships
Every week I will go on a date with my partner. Every day, at a set time, we will talk about the day we have had, and I will listen.

Health
Every week I will make a weekly meal plan, and make a list of healthy, seasonal food. I will eat before I go shopping. Every working day before I go to bed I will prepare a healthy packed lunch for work the next day.

The other thing that you will notice about all of these habits is that they are small, and simple. You will not need to buy anything, or learn anything, or do anything extra. All of these habits work with what you already have. Only set habits that you can do. This way you will not trick yourself into thinking that you need something additional before you can start.

Avoid putting how you feel into your habits. It won't help – in fact it will make it more difficult for your unconscious mind to process. An example of this is if you say I will feel better when I have lost weight. Your unconscious cannot quantify 'better' so will never be able to recognise when you have achieved this feeling. If you put anything into the goal which is a variable, you will be less likely to achieve the goal.

Finally, make sure that each habit that you set will take you closer to your goal *directly*. These must be actions that have a clear and definite intention, and there must be only one intention – your goal.

In the next action I will ask you to create your own list of goal habits. You can think of these as the automated tasks which, once you have set them, will run in your unconscious like a background programme. Once set, and carried out a few times, these habits will become automatic and you will **do them without thinking**.

ACTION

Take fifteen minutes at most and write down a list of
actions (no more than seven) you will do on a daily,
weekly or monthly basis .

When you have done this, use the AMAZE criteria
to challenge each part. Ask yourself the question, is it
Attainable **M**easurable **A**ccurate **Z**oned **E**xact? Keep
going back to the list above to check against it. If it
doesn't fit all of the criteria, change it until it does.
Use the examples given to guide you as well. By the
end of the fifteen minutes, you should have a short
list of actions that fit the AMAZE criteria. If you are
not sure, then less is more.

Finally – write the list out again. Put the actions
into categories:

DAILY
WEEKLY
MONTHLY

Read it through one more time, and put the list
somewhere safe, you will need it later.

Important note: If you try to fit success around the reality
of your life, reality will win out every time. To make this
programme work, you will need to develop habits which
will move you closer to your goal and put your success at
the centre of your life. You are aiming to build habits that

will work for you for the rest of your days, and the only way a habit will develop fully is through repetition, repetition and more repetition. You need to keep plugging away at your new habits at first. After doing them for only three weeks and listening to 'Habits of Success' on the CD, you will no longer have to make any conscious effort to do them. They will now be deeply rooted in your unconscious, requiring no conscious thought or effort.

'Habits of Success'

It's time now to listen to the 'Habits of Success' CD track. The purpose of this track is to take everything you have decided to do to work towards your goal, and put it firmly in the back of your mind. Once it is there you will never be able to trick yourself out of doing these activities again. You will also be carrying out the actions unconsciously, and they will become never-to-be-forgotten habits.

ACTION

Read through your list of 'success habits'.

Go to the toilet if you need to.

Turn off your phone.

Find a time and a place where you can be undisturbed. You can sit down, or lie down, as   >>

---

long as you are comfortable. Do not cross your arms or legs, allow them to relax.

If you wear glasses, take them off.

Now listen to the CD track, 'Habits of Success'.

When the track is over, sit or lie still for a few moments to make sure you are fully reorientated.

NOTE: Remember it is a good idea to have a drink of water after the hypnosis.

Now you have 'fixed' the second part of *becoming amazing* into your unconscious mind. That's enough for today. Do something else. Pick the book up tomorrow. You need to get at least one night's sleep to begin to let this sink in properly. You will start on these actions only when you have completed the programme, so there is no need for you to do anything at all at this point in time. Let the suggestions from the CD sink in.

For now – rest. **You will sleep well tonight.**

Get On With It

Chapter 8

Final preparations before the journey

You now have your list of success habits – the route map to your final destination of *becoming amazing*. Great. Now what?

If the first thought that comes into your mind is, 'That's all very well, but when am I going to find the time to do these things?' you are not alone. A lot of people have a problem getting started on things, and this becomes really obvious when they try to find time to be successful. Some people will do anything rather than take that first step towards success. In this chapter I will take you through all the reasons why people do this, and show you the way to get through it.

Let me start by talking about time. We often talk about time as if it were an entity with the capacity for action of its own: 'time is money', 'time flies', 'time waits for no man'. In fact, as we know logically, time is a constant – something that will pass regardless of what we are doing, or feeling or thinking. How we *feel* about time passing is another matter. One thing that you can be sure of is that once you make a decision to change and to be successful, if you do not get on with it *straight away* then time will seem to speed up. How often have you set yourself a new year resolution, to watch the next year roll in and you haven't rolled out the yoga mat you bought yourself, or even unwrapped the fitness video you sent off for? This is very common, and so easy to sort out.

I cannot begin to tell you how often I heard the excuse (and make no mistake, it is an excuse) *'I don't have the time to...'* made by clients who spend more time talking themselves out of doing things which would make them successful, than they would use if they actually got on and started. Having the time to work on your success is important. Making it a priority is what most people find difficult. So, when people come to me to *be amazing*, and during the process they tell me that they have not found the time to do their success habits, or to get started, I recognise that this is a symptom of something much more basic.

Fact: if what you are setting out to achieve is important enough to you, *you will find the time to do it*. If it is not high enough on your list of priorities then you won't get started on it. So, instead of trying to motivate yourself to get started, what you can do is to focus only on taking the first step that you need to take to get the whole process going.

Just one step. One small step towards success. That's all you will have to take to set the whole process in motion. Before you decide what that step will be for you, I want to talk about that wonderful trick – procrastination. Before I started this programme for myself I was the world's best procrastinator. I would work out what I needed to do, and immediately go and do something else. Kettle-polishing I called it. I would suddenly get engrossed by those little jobs around the house that were neither important, nor urgent – but if I did them then I wouldn't feel guilty about not getting on with the one thing I was supposed to be doing! My drawers were tidy, my CD rack sorted alphabetically, the books in my office straightened. These were not jobs that came under the heading of unfinished business – these were time fillers, nothing more. These are the jobs which you create, and keep creating. The more you do these things, the further away you get from starting on the things which you should be doing – things that move you forward.

So why do people procrastinate?

- **Lack of motivation** If you don't want to do something, you will do anything to avoid starting.

- **Short-term thinking** If you get locked into thinking only about the activity, and not about how it is going to change your life, you will not start.

- **Laziness** If you are plain lazy, and would rather watch the TV than get moving, then you will not start.

- **Comfort zone** If you are quite happy with the way things are at the moment, then you will not start.

You can now see how easy it is to fall into the trap of inertia, and settle for what you have got at the moment, rather than getting what you want out of life. Instead of letting yourself fall into this trap and staying there, while time whizzes past, by the end of this programme you will know what your first step is, and you will be taking it. Your personal reasons for procrastinating will be wiped from your mind by the suggestions in the next hypnosis CD track, so for now – forget about it. Your unconscious mind will deal with this one without you having to think about it, and will make sure **you never trick yourself out of getting started on being a success.**

The action below will help you because it is both preparation and a final bit of procrastination.

ACTION

Take your list of success habits. Schedule them into your diary. (If you have an electronic organiser or computer put them in your calendar as repeating tasks.)

Now they are in your diary as real events. The great thing is that you don't need to start doing them just yet. Putting them in the diary is enough for now. By doing this, starting today, you are making space not only in your day, but also in your mind, and the curious thing is, when you do start to do them, you are now ready to carry out your success habits – without thinking about them. When you have completed the programme, you will action the final component and start the engine of change. When this is done, you will start doing your success habits, naturally and easily – without conscious effort on your part. For now, it is enough to know that there is space in your day to do them. The success habits will be activated when you complete the last action in the book.

Stress

Stress has an unusual role in helping you to *become amazing*. Most people assume that stress is bad and should be avoided, but this is not the full story. In fact, stress is necessary for optimum performance. Too little stress and you will not prepare properly, and too much stress and the adrenalin will interfere with your capacity to do well. Ask any athlete about performing at their best, and they will all agree – you need some stress to do your best.

Stress falls into two categories: one is useful to you, and one is destructive. The first kind, known as immediate stress, is brilliant – it gets your heart racing, focuses your attention on what is happening, and allows you to shut out all distractions. This sort of stress can be very exciting – and if you created the situation which causes the stress, you therefore have control over it. You will use this stress to focus your mind and get you started on the programme, so instead of it being something to avoid and dread, you can and will look forward to it. Creating this type of stress in your life makes you stronger mentally, sharper physically and more able to respond to any situation as it comes to you.

Long-term exposure to stress is a very different matter. Quite simply, it can make you ill. It affects your ability to think. Your behaviour and your judgement become erratic as you respond in an inappropriate way. Your immune system suffers, and you become more prone to illnesses. Long-term exposure to stress is to be avoided, or your response to it needs to be managed better. One of the best-known benefits of hypnotherapy, is that – because it uses relaxation techniques as part of the process – it automatically strengthens your capacity to deal with stress more effectively. When you rest during the hypnosis tracks, you will **let go of any unnecessary nervous tension. Your mind starts to feel clearer and you feel more able to deal with stress.** Enjoying the hypnosis regularly will also help you to become more aware of the things that could stress you, and to find different and more appropriate ways of dealing with that stress.

When it comes to ways of dealing with the negative effects of stress, there are three main approaches. For some people, they need to remove themselves completely from the situation that stresses them. Others need to learn better ways of coping with the stress, and the final group need strategies to interrupt the stress before it becomes damaging to them. Whichever category you fit into, the hypnosis track 'Focus' which you will be prompted to listen to in the next chapter will help you deal with the negative effects of stress more usefully.

On the plus side, how to get the positive stress – the short burst of energy which you will need and will start to enjoy – is also included in the 'Focus' track. This type of stress will heighten your emotions, helping you to learn and remember better and also to become aware of your stressors and your emotional and physical reactions in a way that will help you to use the stress in future.

Stick to the facts – feelings will follow

Why won't it work if I describe feelings and emotions?

I have said before that if you try to represent your goal with feelings, you will fail. Even if you get what you want, you will not feel as you think you ought to feel when you have achieved it. Leave feelings out when you are creating your goal, they are not specific enough for your unconscious mind to make a clear picture from.

Trying to define feelings in clear goal terms only muddies the waters and is too vague and subjective, and so open to interpretation by your unconscious mind. The unconscious part of you needs clarity to really make things happen. Concepts such as 'happier', 'smarter', 'better' and 'well' are not processed by the image-based systems of the brain because they mean something different to everyone. They are based on your own memories of what they mean. Besides, we cannot hold strong emotions long enough to make them useful to this process. If you need some ideas on how to describe your goals, have a look at the examples at the end of the book. In there I have listed a number of the different ways in which people have described their goals. Some people like to put lots of sensory information in there, and others like to keep the descriptions very simple. It really depends on your character.

I know that you will have already imagined how you will feel when you have got your goal – it is only natural. Your positive feelings will come naturally *after* you have achieved your goal, you do not need to define them beforehand, and sometimes they are not the feelings that you initially expected.

There is a well-tested theory behind this. In the 1950s, an aesthetic surgeon called Maxwell Maltz noticed a strange coincidence in patients having surgery to improve their looks. He wrote up the phenomenon in his groundbreaking book, *Pyschocybernetics*. He noticed that when they were questioned after surgery, some of his patients weren't happy with the results. When questioned further, they could not put their finger on what specifically they didn't like, only that the surgery 'had not made them happy'. This is the classic example of pre-deciding how you will feel when you do something to make a change – you very rarely get exactly what you want out of it unless you **describe it clearly and specifically in a way that can be understood by anyone.**

Keep the momentum

Remember why you are doing this programme. You are doing it for you – because there is no time like the present to have the life you want. Keep your goal in mind and refresh your connection with it by daydreaming, if ever you momentarily waver. Keep referring to it as if **it has already happened** and you are waiting to step into that reality. This will keep you focused. This will keep you going if you get tired or stressed. It is still OK. Life happens, remember? Also know that, if you do get overstressed or tired, it is because you are not taking care of yourself properly. Take a step back. Have a rest. Relax. It will do you more good than trying to struggle on. By doing this you are still working towards your goal. Remember that and you will stay on course for success.

Once you have finished the book, you will get on with the first of your actions immediately. It will take around three weeks for the changes to become permanent and unconscious. Your new behaviour will then be a habit to you – the *amazing you*. You will never have to think about success again, it just becomes part of you and the way you act, think and feel from now on. You'll stop being afraid, and will start to recognise when you are getting excited by your life, and begin to revel in it. The question is, are you ready for it? Even if you are not so sure right now – by the end of the programme you will be ready, and raring to get on with it!

Sleep well

Never underestimate the importance of a good night's sleep. Sean Drummond from the University of California, San Diego, who has done extensive research into sleep and brain function says, 'If you have been awake for twenty-one hours straight, your abilities are equivalent to someone who is legally drunk.' Your IQ, your ability to solve problems, plan, learn and concentrate suffer badly. Also, you are less alert and more likely to make mistakes or have accidents. Regular sleep patterns are important. It is better to have regular, shorter nights where you go to bed and wake at the same time, than extended but irregular hours. Sleep does more than give our body a rest, it is also the time when our brain is allowed the freedom to solve problems more laterally. During your REM sleep, your brain can do more than solve problems for you – it can compartmentalise, prioritise and discard *whatever is necessary*. REM sleep allows you to put things to bed – literally, and allows you to be fresh and clear for the next day. For your information, there are three things that will really help you get to sleep. A warm bath, warm drink, or sex. Do not attempt all three at the same time!

No more tricks

There is only one person on earth who can trick you, and that is you. No matter what other people say or do to us, we have a choice about how we respond. This is where confidence in ourselves is the key to keeping on track with our goals. When we feel confident, we look to our own opinion of ourselves, and if someone says or does something which could be hurtful we can ignore it and let it pass by. When we are not feeling confident, words and actions can be harmful, and we retreat into old patterns, and watch our goals slip away.

EXAMPLE

Ruth noticed that if her partner said something negative, she would feel miserable, and respond to this by immediately reaching for the biscuits. When she had eaten them she still felt miserable about >>

---

what had been said, and, worse, she now felt guilty and depressed for eating when she wasn't hungry. Her lack of confidence in dealing with her partner's comment pushed her into repeating a destructive habit.

The first things to recognise here are our mood triggers. You already know the mood that, when you are in it, means your ability to control your behaviour seems to go out the window. A mood trigger is the mood you get into that has a set of behaviours of its own. For example, some people find themselves *automatically* reaching for a cigarette when they become stressed, or bursting into tears when they are angry. Mood triggers set off behaviours which seem out of conscious control.

EXAMPLES
Sad, angry, pre-menstrual, bored

Make a note of your mood triggers.

Mood triggers

When you have listed your mood triggers, the next thing is to change your response to them. You can do this in one of the following ways:

- Take control of what sets the mood off
- Break the connection between the mood and the negative response

If you don't deal with your moods, they can get in the way of your success. Here is how to deal with them. To take control of what sets the mood off, you need to RISE to the occasion.

RECOGNISE THE TRIGGER

INTERRUPT THE CONNECTION

SET OFF IN A DIFFERENT DIRECTION

EXPERIENCE A BETTER MOOD

Easy to say, but how do I make this happen?

You will find the suggestions to make this happen for you later on when you listen to the 'Focus' track on the CD, so you don't need to do anything else at this point. As with all the other suggestions, if mood triggers are not a problem for you, you will ignore those suggestions. Remember, one of the best things about the hypnosis is that you will only accept suggestions which are relevant to you, and will work best for you.

Finally, to break the connection between the mood and the negative habit you can also use what is called a 'pattern breaker'. This is designed to interrupt your thought process just long enough for you to change your response. The easiest one is to imagine a **RED STOP LIGHT** in your mind every time you are in that situation. With the **RED STOP LIGHT** in your mind, the connection between the mood and the response will be interrupted. Do this often enough and the habit will happen less and less, and you will start to feel better about yourself. The mood which kicked it off will also happen less and less as you notice the results of your new habit.

Remember: no one makes you feel anything. How you respond is a choice.

What stopped you before?

I will tell you what stopped you before: quite simply, you did. For whatever reason (and we can all find them if we go looking), you made a decision that there was enough in it for you to stay as you were – and that the benefits of any change were not good enough for you to put the effort in. This is why the key elements of focus, motivation and confidence are run as themes all the way through this programme. Without these in place you might find yourself distracted, or lose momentum, or even fail to believe in yourself the way that you have to if you want to change your life.

I know that I have mentioned this before, but it is important, and one of the things about hypnosis is the use of repetition to 'fix' the information. I want you to remember that:

Without focus – you start your project and then get distracted.

Without confidence – you don't get started because *you* feel you aren't worth the effort.

Without motivation – you either get diverted before you start, you start and soon give up, or you are like a wind-up toy that runs down, getting slower and slower until you stop altogether.

With focus – you always keep an image of why you are doing this in the back of your mind.

With confidence – you believe in yourself, your right to a better life and your ability to get it.

With motivation – you keep on going regardless of what is happening around you, or what obstacles appear.

Apart from when you are prompted in the book, you can use the CD tracks 'Focus', 'Motivation' and 'Confidence' when you have completed the programme. They are there for you whenever you need them – look at them as a form of 'self-medication' if you like – if you need a top-up. After listening to them for a few times you will find that you get to know the words off by heart, and can start repeating them to yourself when you need to – without the CD. You will also find that when you have heard these tracks a few times you will notice **your own inner voice gives these positive suggestions** to keep you on track.

The importance of dreaming

In some esoteric teachings and self-help books it is thought to be enough to have a dream. They say that if you dream hard enough, and want something badly enough, if it is meant to be for you then it will happen. I believe that this is only half of the story. Over the years I have seen many successful people in my practice who are dreamers – in fact they seem to be dreaming of the future all the time, not just when they are sleeping, but each time they have a moment to spare. I am making a clear distinction here: daydreamers dream of a future and do nothing about making it happen – in actual fact, their dreams make them more discontented, as they recognise the difference between what is in their dreams and what is in their lives. Dreamers, however, use the dream to make their goals happen – to motivate themselves. The difference between these dreamers and those who *just* daydream, is that for the successful dreamers their dreams are part of strategic planning.

Many people (including members of the medical professions) believe that our sleep phase, particularly REM sleep, when we dream, is where learned information gets processed and understood. You can see the negative evidence of this theory when you have a bad night's sleep. You wake confused and forgetful and are often clumsy and bad-tempered. This is because you did not have enough good quality sleep to *'put the day to bed'*, and so you end up trying to juggle information consciously when it should be resting at the back of your mind where you can get to it when you need it.

You may have experienced this when you were stressed in the past. If the stress causes you to sleep badly, then – when you wake – the cause of the stress keeps coming back into your thoughts, even though there is nothing you can do about it at that moment. It seems that when you don't process information fully in your sleep, your unconscious processing system keeps bringing it to the front of your mind, no matter how irrelevant it is to what you are doing, as a way of reminding you to deal with it. This can create a backlog of information to be dealt with, and we can get to a point where we can't take any more information on board – so we get bogged down with the day-to-day information, just dealing with the minimum of what is in front of our noses.

So what is so different about dreamers?

Well, dreamers unconsciously use their REM sleep to create and refine their future image of how life will be when they have achieved their goal. When they sleep, when they dream, they are dreaming of life from inside their future. They are dreaming this new life *as if they are already living there*. It is almost like a parallel universe to them. Each time they revisit the dream it changes a little – refinements occur. This is important, because when you do this, you are improving your goal each time, creating more and more memories of your future, with increased numbers of sensory connections. Your unconscious mental processes really are incredible – it is like having a computer with a background program running while you are working. You monitor it occasionally, but it is quite happy to run its course and do the work without you having to intervene.

One thing your unconscious cannot do is make a distinction between past, present and future – and this creates an unusual tension in the mind between what is going on outside (reality) and what is going on in your thoughts (the goal). Successful dreamers are aware of this tension, and this is one of the main things that motivates them. When they live in their dreams, they are so happy and contented that reality becomes paler and more dull – and this spurs them on to action every time. Their dreams turn into reality because in their minds the goal already is real – it already exists for them – it creates excitement and adrenelin – and pushes them forward at an incredible rate. So remember: dreaming is good as long as it spurs you into action.

Why is it important to be so detailed when setting the goal?

I talk quite a bit in this programme about people tricking themselves out of success. Like the pact between Dr Faustus and the Devil, if you leave a loophole in your goal, your conscious mind will be able to find ways of talking you out of making the change and into maintaining the status quo. Never underestimate how clever we are at tricking ourselves into doing nothing. Another reason for being so inclusive is to make the mental image as strong and clear as possible. The stronger it is, the more easily you will work towards it without conscious effort.

Get this part right, and everything else falls easily into place. By the end of the next chapter you will have created the right type of image which will focus your attention and motivate you towards your goal, and you will have the confidence to go for it. When you know what you *really* want, how to get it, and how to get started will become much clearer too, as the unconscious part of your mind will start working these other elements out for you **without you even trying**.

Chapter 9
Real life

Get focused and stay focused

I used to find it really frustrating when I read self-help books and they talked about making changes, and developing strategies, and creating tools, that they very rarely talked about *how* to make it fit in with what is already going on in your life. One of the major differences with this programme is that it does take into consideration real life – jobs, family, stress – and builds success around it. 'Be Amazing' works with these things, accepts that we all have responsibilities and other commitments, and helps you build your success into the life you have already. Everyone knows it is easy to lose weight if you go away to a health farm, or to make a decision about starting a new business if you forget that you have a family. 'Be Amazing' incorporates success into your life by allowing you to recognise that there will be times when other things are more urgent and important than the programme, and then by helping you to get back on track if you have to take a break, rather than using the break as an excuse to stop.

'Be Amazing' is about you, only you – about your life, your dreams, your plans. It seems so ironic to me that as we grow up and real life takes over, most of us find it easier to settle for what we have than to push ourselves to achieve our dreams. Ask a healthy child what they want to be when they grow up and they will tell you about the exciting life that they are planning. Ask an adult what they want out of life, and so many of them seem to be just going along for the ride.

There is another point I would like to make here, and that is the number of people who think that something like winning the lottery will sort out their problems. I have news for those people: winning the lottery may solve some old problems, but it brings with it a whole set of new problems. Think about it. Who do you tell? Who do you share your money with? Do you trust people who suddenly appear in your life now you have money? The list goes on. Now you could call these 'superior' problems – but what is it that people really want from winning the lottery? Financial security, happiness, freedom, etc. The chances of winning the lottery are smaller than the chances of being hit by a piece of meteor debris, so get real.

However, you can create *all* of these events, if they are part of your goal, by using the techniques in the 'Be Amazing' programme – it is within your grasp. The last change you need to create to kick it all off is to change your attitude. You need to believe that you have a right to be successful. The only question is: Are you ready to believe in yourself?

To answer this, let me ask you another question: Have you ever been in two minds about something? On one hand you want to get a new job, and on the other you start to add up all the reasons why you should stay in the one you have. I bet you have gone round and round in circles and then ended up so confused that inertia sets in and so you do absolutely nothing about the situation. 'Be Amazing' gets both of your two minds talking to each other – with the end result that you stop fooling yourself, start making changes and getting on with life, with both your unconscious and your conscious mind working together to achieve your goal. You stop fooling yourself into thinking that this is all there is, and that you are fine as you are. I will say it again – you wouldn't be reading this book if you were honestly happy with your life as it is now.

The other big difference between 'Be Amazing' and other programmes is it recognises that everyone has days when they are not happy with what they have, and days when they get even more miserable about what they don't have. 'Be Amazing' is a programme which lets you take time off, and still be working towards your goal, without beating yourself up about it. Ask an athlete about the importance of taking time out to rest, or the crop farmer about the importance of letting a field lie fallow – there are times when *doing absolutely nothing at all* is a real part of success. Recognising when to work and when to rest will become a theme in your life from now on, and you will stop tricking yourself into thinking that once you have taken a break, you might as well give up. By now you are really clear on the mind games you used to play that stopped your success before. Above all, you are now well on the way to getting the life you want. You have given yourself a kick up the backside to get started, the strategies to keep going, and a goal to inspire you. More than that, you have created a habit for success which will work for you not only with this goal – but all your future projects.

The changes in you are now *unconscious*; they are so subtle, you probably haven't yet noticed how these changes are happening. They needed to become unconscious for this to work – so by the end of the book you don't even notice that you are doing things differently, better. Because of this you won't be tempted to trick yourself – you couldn't even if you tried. As the hypnosis suggestions kick in ever more strongly with each CD track you listen to, you begin to notice that change gets easier and easier because you can't fool yourself any more if you try to backtrack or make excuses.

On a related note, in all my years of experience using hypnosis to help people change, I have learned one unavoidable truth: there is not an adult out there who is content with every aspect of their lives – striving for something better is part of human nature. By now you will know if you were someone who went to great lengths to explain why you lived your life the way you did, and so justified why you were *not* going to change. You may have discovered that you were at the other end of the scale – creating your own problems where there were none before. Whichever you *were* – you are now different. This programme has stopped you fooling yourself into believing that you have no control over changing things once and for all. If you have learned only one thing, the fact that we *all* have choices, it will have gone a long way to changing your mind about your potential.

I am too busy to do the things which will change my life

When I am working one-on-one with clients this is one of the phrases I hear most often, or a variation on it.

EXAMPLES

My job takes up most of my time.

I have a family and have to spend time with them.

I have social commitments.

I have elderly parents who need my attention.

As I constantly point out to these people *successful people have lives too*! The difference between them and anyone else is that they do not use them as an excuse for failing to achieve. Instead, they use them as ways of motivating them to do something about their lives. I will use the same examples to demonstrate what I mean, and the difference here is not money – it is attitude.

EXAMPLES

My job takes up most of my time – **so I am going to get a new job which will not be so all-consuming**.

I have a family and have to spend time with them – **so I will change my life so that they become central to my plans and I can spend even more time with them**.

I have social commitments – **while I am pursuing my goal I will put them to one side, so that I will enjoy them even more when I have achieved my goal.**

I have elderly parents who need my attention – **and because I want to give them the best care I can, I will look after my own health and well-being to make sure I can always help them.**

Now you can see what I mean. You are **not** too busy, but you are locked into a form of self-sabotage.

This happens for one of the following reasons:

- You are using your full schedule as an excuse to stay as you are.
- Your full schedule causes you so much stress that you cannot even think about success.
- You are failing to see that when you *become amazing*, you will have all the time you want to do the things you want to do, or feel that you need to do.
- You do not feel that it is important enough for you to change your life, or these things would not be considerations.

Another thing for those who are too busy to make change is the fact that you now have to acknowledge that you do have choices. The real issue here is that you have got so locked into your habits and routines that you believe the *way* you do things is the only way, and you can't **imagine doing things differently**. It is time to stop the tricks once and for all, and the worst of these tricks is being 'too busy'.

When people talk about being 'too busy', what they mean is that their time is already filled up with activities and actions, and because they have done these things for a long time, they have got into routines. You know the sort of thing I mean here, things you feel that you *have* to do, *ought* to do and *must* do.

Do you remember in Chapter 3 when I talked about 'no compromise' areas of your life? Just think for a moment, if you lost your health, or your family, or your self-respect. *A lot of the elements of your life that you thought were SO important then become meaningless.* You don't *have* to do the job you are doing, you don't *have* to visit friends and go out socialising, you don't *have* to run from one place to another looking after other people. YOU MAKE A CHOICE to do these things – and when you take a step back and look at the things you feel that you have to do, they are purely habit, and, if you do still *want* to do them, you can look at better ways of doing them – ones which will allow you then to work successfully towards your goal.

ACTION

List all the things which you feel that you *have* to do on a daily, weekly and monthly basis. Take fifteen minutes at most to do this.

Now refer back to your own personal areas of 'no compromise'.

You will find that most of the things on the list are not things that you *have* to do, but things that you *choose* to do. Once you accept this, you will find that you can and will find different ways of doing these things if you still want to do them:

■ You will realise that there are a number of things on the list that you no longer want to do, they are just habit.

- You will immediately feel less stressed as you realise that **you do have a choice about the way you do things.**

EXAMPLE

Brian has a house with a mortgage, a wife and two young children. He was in a job that he hated, but felt that he had to do the job because it provided for his family. What Brian wanted to do was to spend quality time with his family, and be more relaxed about life. He worked through the programme and reassessed his priorities – did he want to be a happier, healthier, more hands-on father or one who was always in a hurry and stressed? He worked through, with his wife, a practical strategy. They downsized, and now his wife works part-time, giving Brian more time with his family. He is currently working on a project to renovate houses in partnership with his brother as a different way of financing their lifestyle. The whole family is now more settled and happier with the new arrangement.

I don't want people to think I am selfish

It is inevitable that when you change and develop, especially if those people around you have not changed in that time, you might find yourself accused of being selfish. Selfish because you are not fulfilling *their* needs any more. Shakespeare said: 'Self-love is not so vile a sin as self-neglecting', and, boy, are some of us good at neglecting ourselves. See if you recognise yourself in the following description:

Some people spend half their waking lives running around for other people, trying to help and please them. If this is you, take a step back for the moment. If the person you are trying to help genuinely likes and cares about you, and you then tell them that you are trying to do something truly amazing to improve your life – *if they really care about you, they will support and encourage you.* If all that other person sees is what they might lose when you change, they are only interested in themselves. You can then allow yourself to take a mental step back from that relationship, because whatever you do for yourself you are not going to please them.

Throughout all of the hypnosis tracks there are suggestions to help you become more confident in yourself and, where necessary, more assertive. I have also worked with clients to create some set phrases to use to help them to change their situation.

EXAMPLES OF PHRASES

For a son with an elderly mother

I am getting a new job which will mean that I will be moving further away. I know that you will be pleased for me because I will be much happier in this new job.

>>

For the mother who did everything for her son (now twenty-two)
You will not be able to bring your laundry to me any more, I won't have time to do it as I am starting a part-time course. You said that you wanted me to enjoy myself, so now I am learning French – isn't it fantastic!

For the wife who never saw her husband because he was always working
I have decided to start a part-time job, that way you won't have to do so much overtime and we can spend more time together like you always wanted.

For the woman who wanted to lose weight and has an insecure partner.
I am going on this diet so you can feel proud of your sexy girlfriend when you take me out.

These phrases are called 'simple binds', and they place the person who is listening into a position where they can only respond in one way – the way you are steering them to respond. If they don't, they show that they do not have your best interests at heart.

There are two keys to making these types of phrases work for you.

First, by taking what someone else has said in the past, such as 'I only want you to be happy', and including it in the phrase when you tell them what you are doing. When you do this, you are showing them that by changing your life you are doing what *they wanted you to do*! Now, if they were lying about wanting you to be happy, or were only paying lip-service to your needs because it suited them at the time, they will not be happy that you have changed. However, *they will not be able to say anything about it without then making themselves a liar*. This leaves you free from any guilt that they might otherwise have tried to put on to you about feeling neglected in any way. You are guilt-free because you can recognise they were more interested in their needs than yours.

Second, when you declare your intentions in this particular way you are giving the people around you a choice. They have a choice to change with you, and support you – and ultimately benefit from the change. Remember, when people around you get disturbed by your change it might not be that they do not want you to be successful, it may be that they are afraid that they will lose something. So help them to support you. If they don't want to, that is their problem, and a choice that they make. Knowing this, you can **make your changes with a clear conscience**.

I want you to be really clear on something at this point: when you use language to guide other people into responding in a certain way, it will only work if, by doing so, the other person benefits in the end. Going back to the examples I have given you, I will demonstrate what I mean by giving you the subtext to each.

EXAMPLES OF PHRASES

For a son with an elderly mother

I am getting a new job which will mean that I will be moving further away. I know that you will be pleased for me because I will be much happier in this new job.

Subtext: If I am happy, you will be happy too, so when we see each other we will have a nice time together.

For the mother who did everything for her son (now twenty-two)

You will not be able to bring your laundry to me any more, I won't have time to do it as I am starting a part-time course. You said that you wanted me to enjoy myself, so now I am learning French – isn't it fantastic!

Subtext: You want me to enjoy myself. Now I am, so you will be pleased because I took your advice.

For the wife who never saw her husband because he was always working

I have decided to start a part-time job, that way you won't have to do so much overtime and we can spend more time together like you always wanted.

Subtext: If you really want to spend more time with me and this will allow us to do so, you will support me in this decision. >>

> *For the woman who wanted to lose weight and has an insecure partner*
> I am going on this diet so you can feel proud of your sexy girlfriend when you take me out.
> **Subtext: My new look and confidence will be a reflection on you, and it will make you look better.**

In all of these phrases, the subtext is always that there is an advantage for the person listening *if they support you in the changes you are making*. When you start using language to guide people around you to help you make your changes, you find that their attitude changes, and your life gets easier and easier.

Habits

In Chapter 7 I talked you through the habits and patterns that you have now created which will move you towards *becoming amazing*. You have many other habits too, and in this chapter I want to talk about these.

ACTION

Draw a line down the middle of a page. At the top of the left-hand column write DANGER, and at the top of the right-hand column write SAFE. Take ten >>

minutes, no more, and list your habits under the relevant headings. Remember – a habit in this context is something you do *without thinking*.

Example

DANGER	*SAFE*
I procrastinate	*I am organised*
I get stressed before I have to do something new	*I plan ahead*
I put other people before myself	*When I focus I get the job done*

Making these lists will help you recognise that you have lots of habits – some useful and some not so useful.

ACTION

Take a deep breath and let it go. Focus your attention on the DANGER list, and read each one out loud. When you have read one, close your eyes, and imagine a **RED STOP LIGHT** suddenly coming on in front of you. Open your eyes and do the same with the next one and the next one, until you have gone all the way through the DANGER list.   >>

Once again, take a deep breath and let go. Now, focus your attention on the SAFE list. When you have read the first one off this list, close your eyes and imagine a **GREEN GO LIGHT** coming on in front of you. Open your eyes and do the same with the next one and the next until you have gone all the way through the SAFE list.

What you have now done is set a trigger – so the next time you are about to activate any one of these habits, your unconscious mind will decide whether it is SAFE or DANGER for you to do it. After around – you guessed it – three weeks, the only habits that will be getting through will be the ones which are safe for you. This does not mean that you will suddenly be like a robot, only doing the things which move you on to your goal. What it does mean is that you will be more focused and relaxed, and less likely to trick yourself out of success. All the way through the hypnosis CD are suggestions to help 'fix' good habits into your mind, so you do not need to think about how this will happen – your unconscious mind is about to take over on this one and **you will have habits of success that will last you a lifetime.**

A little and often makes the programme work

It is far too easy to get distracted by real life, and overwhelmed by the whole idea of changing. In fact, it is so much easier to look at your goal and say, 'I'm too busy right now, there is too much going on in my life at the moment.' Then your dreams and plans drift, and get overtaken by other considerations, and other people.

You probably know the expression 'eating the elephant slice by slice', meaning to break down something huge and overwhelming into small and manageable pieces. Remember, by breaking the programme into small sections, and doing only one small section at a time, you will get through it effortlessly. This in turn shows you how to break the process into small sections, habits, thoughts, behaviours – and get to grips with each one, effortlessly, so that you become this *amazing you* without being aware of any conscious effort. This way the changes will stick – for ever. By breaking it down into small, manageable pieces it becomes practically effortless – and this way you are much more likely to get started, keep going, and get what you want.

So now you know: to get through this programme, choose to do just a little at a time, as and when you want, and how you want. It will just become a habit to read, listen or carry out the actions in these pages.

ACTION

Get your diary, and make an appointment with yourself daily to work on some aspect of your programme. This appointment is not to be changed or moved around – think of it as an appointment with your future, and the more often you keep the appointment, the more real your future becomes.

Now it is time to listen to another hypnosis track on the CD. This is the 'Focus' track, and you can do this as often as you like while you are doing the programme, but make sure that it is on a day when you are not listening to any of the other tracks. It is important that you give your mind time to absorb one set of suggestions without confusion.

ACTION

Go to the toilet if you need to.

Turn off your phone.

Choose a time and find a place where you can be undisturbed. You can sit down, or lie down, as long as you are comfortable. Do not cross your arms or legs, allow them to relax.

If you wear glasses, take them off. >>

Now listen to the 'Focus' track on the CD.

When the track is over, sit or lie still for a few moments to make sure you are fully reorientated.

Remember: if anything happens that needs your attention while you are listening to the CD, you will become fully alert and able to respond. Afterwards you can continue where you left off.

Chapter 10
The first step

Everything you have done so far has been focused on preparation – on knowing exactly what you want and how to get it, and on the confidence, motivation and focus to do all these things. You have not, yet, got started.

I want to introduce you to the final – and one of the cruellest – tricks your mind can play on you. You clear the decks, you plan, you get organised, and then you don't start. Instead, you procrastinate and say to yourself, 'I have everything in place, so I can start when I like.' You allow yourself to get distracted, and suddenly notice that the bedroom needs decorating, or you haven't had a holiday in a while and that you 'had better do that now, because if you don't, then you won't have time, what with working towards my goal, and all'. Recognise it? We all know people who say that they will stop smoking after Christmas, or lose weight after their holiday. There will always be another obstacle to getting started – *if you look for it*. In this final stage of the programme you are going to focus on recognising that the last hurdle is all in the mind. This chapter examines this final hurdle, and gets you to jump over it once and for all.

Why go looking for excuses not to start when I have done most of the work already?

- fear of success
- fear of failure

What sort of people fail at this point?

- people who get afraid
- people who listen to the complainers
- people who go looking for unfinished business
- people who wait too long to jump in

I have already covered these areas in previous chapters, so you already know the theories. This is where you finally put them into practice.

When you have read this last chapter, you are going to do the final action. Right there and then – specifically when you have finished the last page of this book. Let me tell you why it is so important that you do this. All of the suggestions in the programme have been building up to this moment – the moment you complete the book. The suggestions have gathered momentum, and will push you to complete the final action. When you respond to the final suggestions you will trigger a cascade of all the previous suggestions that you took on board, through the actions, the CD tracks and everything you have read in these pages. The sooner you finish the book, the quicker you start on *becoming amazing*, the faster you *become amazing*, the sooner you will get the benefits.

All well and good, but I will just do this first …

No – you won't. If you do anything else between finishing the book and getting on with it you break the pattern. I know that there will always be unfinished business that you could do before starting a new project. Do you really *have* to do it first? If this is honestly the case, then go back to your list of success habits and create space in your schedule to action periodically the jobs that you used to use as excuses *not* to start. Make space and time for those jobs in your success habits. You might find that when it comes to actually doing those jobs, you will realise that they were not so important, or even urgent, and you may even be able to delegate them to someone else. Don't get me wrong, we all have unfinished business. There will never be a day when you have completely cleared everything that you have to do – life just isn't like that.

To get this really clear in your mind, once and for all, I'm going to clarify what unfinished business *really* is. There are three main types. First, the things that you really need to do, and for whatever reason have not got around to. Second, the jobs that you 'meant to get round to' but never found time. Finally, there are the one-off tasks that you know will start the whole success ball rolling – the things you could do if you wanted to.

In the first type of unfinished business are the jobs like filing your paperwork. You know it needs to be done, and that it will not take much time, but the longer you leave it, the bigger the job becomes, and the more you avoid it. These jobs do not move you any closer to achieving your goal, but they will take up space in your mind and make you anxious and concerned if you do not do them. Creating space in your success habits schedule to do things that in themselves are not directly related to getting your goal, but will help you focus when they are done, is really important.

EXAMPLE

Bella wanted to run her own interior design business. She desperately wanted to get started on finding a course, but she had a project on at work which meant that she was having to bring work home. She felt that she couldn't get started on her own business because she had to do work for the job she was in, and hated.

By doing the programme, Bella realised that her avoidance of the work project was actually causing her to postpone the day when she could get up and running with her own company. So instead of using up her time and effort in resenting and avoiding the >>

> *project, she threw herself into it during working hours, got it finished and started looking for her course. By seeing the work project as part of her progress to success rather than an obstacle, she could get past it and move into a more successful frame of mind.*

This is the unfinished business which you will prioritise. Recognise that by getting these things out of the way they will have a role in your future – it moves you closer to your goal, so schedule into your success habits tasks that are in themselves not related to the goal, but would get in your way if you didn't do them.

If you need to prioritise other work, the easiest way to do it is to put ten minutes aside at the end of your working day, or some other natural punctuation point (as part of your bedtime preparation, for example), and make a list of no more than seven items of 'things to do'. When you have done this, you will periodically action them throughout the next day, and enjoy drawing a line through each one on the list as you do it. Only put things on a list that you can do in that day, like 'buy paint' or 'phone brother', not 'write novel' or 'paint picture'. If you put these on a list they will only create anxiety. Instead, put 'write two pages of novel', or 'spend one hour filling in the sky on my painting' and you will get the book written and the painting completed – effortlessly.

The second type of unfinished business consists of jobs that have been hanging around for ever, and are neither enjoyable, nor are they important to you. That is why you have not done them yet. These are things which you may perhaps have started, but not completed. You may have put a lot of time, effort or even money into the project – it seemed like a good idea at the time – but now recognise that this has become an obstacle to your goal. You are never going to complete it. It is blocking up your thought processes as you feel guilty about not having finished it.

Draw a line under it. Let it go.

When I was working through this section of the programme for myself, and I started to look at the unfinished business around me, I found half of a patchwork quilt which I had started when I was fourteen! I had hung on to it because somewhere in the back of my mind was the idea that I might, one day, finish it. It went straight in the bin – and the relief I felt was unbelievable. I no longer had to worry about when I was going to get round to it.

You have unfinished business which it is time to discard. This is the time to recognise what these jobs are, and to junk them. The relief will be fantastic – your mind will be clearer, and you will feel as if a weight has been lifted from your mind – and it has.

The final type of unfinished business consists of the easy-to-do, one-off jobs which, when you do them, will move you forward. These are the phone calls, or the letters, or the rewrite of your CV. These are the jobs that will start you on the road to *becoming amazing*. These can be the hardest to action, because we know the implications of doing these things. We know that when we do that one thing – there is no going back. These one-off jobs that kick-start the process of change are thought of as unfinished business because we could *already have done them*. These are the jobs you 'could have', 'should have' and 'would have' got round to *'if only …'*.

This is the unfinished business for you to compartmentalise. What I mean by this is that you will, mentally, put them into a clear mental box where they exist outside of your daily life. You will not compare them with any of the other jobs that you have to do, because they are a one-off. These are the things that you will do at the end of this book. You will get on with it *without even thinking*.

There was a lot of unfinished business in my life, as there probably is in yours right now, but once I understood how this unfinished business would impact on my life, it allowed me to sort out which things I needed to action, and how. When there is something which you should have done, could have done, and have *not* done – then you can always find a reason why you haven't done it if you go looking for it. It is important not to become overwhelmed by the goal – in the end you are only ever doing one thing at a time. Don't worry – the hypnosis will help you with this too.

ACTION

Take ten minutes and list all the jobs which you should have, could have or would have finished. Put the list under three headings:

THINGS I AM NEVER GOING TO DO
Admit to yourself the jobs/ideas that have been hanging around for ever, and put them under this heading.

THINGS TO GO IN SUCCESS HABITS
Put the jobs that are not relevant to your goal, but that you need to action regularly to keep moving forward towards your goal.

THINGS TO DO NOW
Put down the one-off actions that will start you off on your goal.

EXAMPLES

NEVER GOING TO DO
Learn Russian
Go to the gym
Finish the novel I started ten years ago

>>

> *TO GO IN SUCCESS HABITS*
> *Do filing*
> *Telephone family weekly*
> *Arrange to meet friends*
>
> *TO DO NOW*
> *Make an appointment to meet X*
> *Write my CV*
> *Get kit ready for first swimming session*

ACTION

Now, take the first list – 'THINGS I AM NEVER GOING TO DO' – and tear it up. Shred it. Burn it if you want to. Destroy it completely – and *let those ideas go*, they only held you back.

Take the second list – 'THINGS TO GO IN SUCCESS HABITS' and schedule them into your daily, weekly or monthly diary.

With the third list – 'THINGS TO DO NOW' – check that they are one-off events. Check too that they are relevant to your goal. This action or these actions are the ignition keys to your new life.

The actions from the final group are the things that only need to be done once. A phone call, an email, a bag made ready for the first trip to the gym. You will do this action when you have read to the end of my chapter and listened to the final hypnosis CD track. You are nearly there now.

Silence is golden

In other sections of the book, I have advised that you talk to people close to you about what you are doing, keeping them informed. In this section I need to let you know that there will be times when it is better to keep what you are doing to yourself – and not to talk about it to *anyone*. There are sound reasons for this:

- Other people will start giving you advice, which can be confusing and put you off.
- If you talk about it with others, you can start to talk yourself out of it more easily.
- And on the positive side, you make stronger *unconscious* connections in the brain.

This is the process: when you tell other people that you are doing something which they do not know anything about, they will, quite naturally, want to give you their opinion! That's all very well, but other people's opinions about how you should be running your life will not help you. Ironically, the worst of those people are the ones who 'mean well' when they give you their advice. They are often people who care about you, and the advice will be given in such a way that it would seem rude for you not to listen. You can sometimes miss an undercurrent of negativity that goes with it, so it slips through and gets to you. Be very wary of people who start their sentences with 'You know I mean well …'. You will end up walking away from your encounter feeling less happy, and often quite irritated that you told them in the first place – and it will set in motion a thought process which can cause you to lose momentum or get disheartened.

Decide whether to tell someone what you are doing based on how good you feel about yourself at that time. If you are not feeling completely secure, stay quiet. When you are secure in yourself, you can tell as many people as much as you like about what you are doing, because their opinions will never harm, only motivate you. Remember, unasked for advice is *not* advice, it is only someone else's opinion.

EXAMPLE

Anna came to see me to help her stop smoking. She left the session perfectly calm and confident that she would never smoke again. She then went home and told her partner that she had been to a hypnotherapist to stop smoking. He told her that he had read in a newspaper of a woman who saw a hypnotherapist to stop smoking and she put on loads of weight as a result. This set off a train of thought that wasn't there before, and Anna started smoking soon afterwards because she was so afraid that this would happen to her too.

Recognise the scenario? It is always better for your progress to avoid this by not telling people what you are planning to do. Wait until you have already done it, and they notice the changes in you. Then you will be confident enough that if they do start to give you their opinion, it will not affect you in any negative way. In fact, you can use it as a way of motivating you *because* the changes are noticeable to others now. Leaving it for them to notice also tells you a lot about your relationship with them – if it takes them a while to notice that you are changing, then they are not really as aware of you as you might have thought. Remember, relationships will always be affected when you change.

Another group of advice givers are those who really don't want you to change. These are easier to spot and they will very quickly tell you that what you are about to try will not work. They then go on to give you as many reasons as they can to explain to you why it is much better for you to stay as you are.

EXAMPLE

Ruth came to see me to lose weight. She realised that food wasn't really the issue. Her problem was that she drank too much alcohol and didn't do enough exercise. Using hypnosis I helped start her on a fitness and alcohol-free programme to kick-start her metabolism. During this time, her friends kept >>

---

calling her to come out in the evening – and said that she had 'got really boring' since starting the programme. Ruth went out with them, to be told that she 'had to have a drink' with them. Ruth was not confident enough to lose this group of friends, and so she started drinking again that evening, and by the morning felt hung-over, fat (because she had also gone for a curry afterwards), and a total failure. Her so-called 'friends' had become obstacles to her success.

Working through the programme and building up her confidence, she realised that these people were not friends in the true sense of the word – they did not care about her, they were more interested in themselves and their fun. Ruth focused on getting fit and losing weight, and used the fact that these people were not really interested in her as a way of finding new, more positive people to fill her life with. She did just that, and now has control over her weight, and has just got engaged.

Both the 'well meaners' and those people who want you to stay the same (false friends) have a common problem. The problem is themselves. They will view your goals and objectives in the light of their own insecurities. If they feel that they aren't prepared to put in the effort themselves to change their lives, they will try to talk you out of making changes. That way, they feel better for not having made the changes in their lives which they know that they should make. If you don't change, it justifies the fact that they don't have to change either. You know now that **you are responsible for your own destiny** – no one can *make* you do anything that you do not want to do ever again. **You have a choice as to how you respond in future.**

As well as the times when you decide to stay silent about what you are doing, you need to make time for inner silence too. Taking time out to have a peaceful moment is so important, especially when you are working towards a goal. If you do not do this, there is a danger that you may start feeling overwhelmed. Allow yourself times to do nothing. Remember, this is an essential part of success. If you don't take time out for yourself already, put it in your success habits. It is during the times of inner silence that you will find the answers to problems.

ACTION

Switch off anything that could disturb you, such as your phone.

Light a candle* and focus on the flame.

When you have the image of that flame clear and bright in your mind, blow out the candle and　　>>

close your eyes. You will continue to see the light, even though your eyes are closed, and you can focus on that.

Concentrate on your breathing and focus on allowing yourself to breathe deeply and well, letting your body relax on each out-breath. Count down from ten to one, using your out-breath as a guide when you count.

Continue to focus on the light, and imagine that in that light is your goal. You can hear, see and feel how it will be when you can step into that light. Try to bring the sights, sound and sensations closer to you. Spend as long as you like enjoying the sensations.

Bring yourself back to the present by counting up from one to ten, counting up on your in-breath, bringing all those exciting feelings with you, and becoming progressively more energised as you bring yourself fully alert.

* To supplement the memory state of success, I have a designed a signature **SUCCESS** candle which has an aroma of sweet almond, said to attract money and good fortune, and frankincense, which is thought to invoke strength of conviction. Details of how to get a **SUCCESS** candle can be found at the end of the book. Whenever you light the candle, even when you are not doing self-hypnosis, the scent will trigger feelings of calm and remind you of your goal.

Light the blue touchpaper

It requires bravery to take the first step. Bravery to recognise that what you are about to do will change the way you live your life, and your future.

This is not a time for calculation, and weighing up the pros and cons of what you are about to do – now is the time for action. There is no *right* time to *become amazing* – there is only now. Once you feel this, as you will when you have completed the programme, you will never look back, except to see how far you have come in such a short space of time.

Bravery comes when you recognise that what you are doing is **what you could always have done**, but just needed that extra 'something' to give you the push in the right direction. This programme is that extra push. With the suggestions that you have already heard you will start to feel **more confident, more motivated and more focused.** Now all you have to do is take that first step. If the thought of doing so makes your heart beat a little faster, good – remember, it is excitement, not fear. If the thought of getting started doesn't excite you, go back and check – have you made your goal big enough, clear enough, specific enough? Maybe you need to **dream a little more, make your future brighter and more exciting.** Each time you go through this programme, setting new goals, your confidence will grow and you will push yourself a little further each time – and it feels wonderful. Enjoy it.

Get started

It is time, at last, to carry out the last component of the 'Be Amazing' programme. In this last part you will pull the whole process together. You have your goal in mind. You have taken on board suggestions for confidence. You have worked out the success habits to take you there, and unconsciously picked out the suggestions from the CD tracks that best motivate you. Finally, you have now focused on making the first step, the step which will set all the other elements in motion.

Now you will listen to the final 'Be Amazing' CD track. The purpose of this track is to take everything you have decided to do in order to work towards your goal, and put it firmly in the back of your mind. Once it is there you will never be able to trick yourself out of completing these activities again. You will also be carrying out the success habits unconsciously, and from now on you will never forget them. Your goal will be safely in the back of your mind where no one can tamper with it – including you. Once you have listened to this final track there is no going back. **You are ready for success.**

As usual, you do not need to think about how this will happen, because the suggestions to pull this whole programme together will be made to you in the final CD track. You will have noticed by now that the more you listen to the hypnosis, the more comfortable you become, and the more benefit you get from the relaxation. You may also have felt as if there were times when you seemed to drop off to sleep. This only happened because you were comfortable with what was being said. By now, you are completely at ease with the hypnotic state. You will get the most significant benefit of all from the final audio track, so enjoy it.

ACTION

Remind yourself of what your first step will be.

Go to the toilet if you need to.

Turn off your phone.

Find a time and a place where you can be undisturbed. You can sit down, or lie down, as long as you are comfortable. Do not cross your arms or legs, allow them to relax.

If you wear glasses, take them off.

Now listen to the CD track, 'Get Started'.

When the track is over, sit or lie still for a few moments to make sure you are fully reorientated.

Now you have 'fixed' the final part of *becoming amazing* into your unconscious mind, you are primed and ready.

Fine – but how will I know that it has worked?

Now you have completed the programme, you are a different person. You can no longer trick or fool yourself into old, pointless patterns of thoughts or actions like you used to. This, I have to warn you, can sometimes become pleasantly annoying. Like having a smarter, more successful version of you constantly nudging at you all the time towards the future. Actually, this is what has now happened. In your mind you have created (and have just installed with the final hypnosis track) a new version of you in your brain. This image contains your dream and your goal, the success habits that will take you there, and the final element – your first step to change. When you have completed the last action and read the last line of the book, the image will be activated. When this happens, your brain will stimulate you with sufficient stress to excite you, and then you will get on with making the changes in your life – unconsciously. You are about to take the last step to *becoming amazing*, and now you are fully prepared for it. All the arrangements have been made, and part of your mind has already completed the journey to success. Part of your thoughts are already there, in the future, in the time when you have completed the process – pre-living your life, your goal. This part of your mind is active in your sleep, in your dreams, constantly coaxing you forward from now on to start living your future – now. These dreams will keep giving you the focus, motivation and confidence you want, *whenever you need it.* **From now on you are in control. Make the decision to be successful and it can all be yours.** *Being amazing* is not just a one-off event, it is a template for life, and now this is exactly what you have become. Congratulations. You are about to take the final step to *becoming amazing.*

Life is for living

So, finally, about time…
        One more step, just one more…

ACTION
When you put the book down, when you have read the last word, I have one final suggestion for you:

TAKE THE FIRST STEP.

WRITE THAT LETTER.

MAKE THAT PHONE CALL.

BOOK THAT FLIGHT.

…JUST DO IT NOW.

Enjoy the journey…
All the very best to you, Ursula James.

Examples

Examples

I have put together a few examples of the type of useful first steps, success habits and ultimate goals which have been commonly used by my clients. You might find these helpful when you create your own.

As you will notice, some of the ideas are more specific than others – this is just to give you an idea of the range of variations in how different people think. Also note that there are a number of first steps and ultimate goals for each, even though you will only need one.

- Weight control
- Relationship success
- Running a marathon
- Career
- Fertility
- Writing a book
- Stopping smoking
- Learning a language

Weight control

First step

Throw out 'fat' clothes

Create a timetable of how much weight I want to lose each week so I know when I will have lost the total amount

Throw out my scales

Stick picture of myself looking at my worst on to the fridge door

Dig out the skirt I want to fit into and put it at the front of my wardrobe

Join weight-loss club

Success habits

- Weekly food shopping
- Walk daily
- Swim three times a week
- Put on disco music while doing housework, and have fun dancing
- Mark off on calendar each pound I lose
- Go to meetings of weight-loss club
- Do something every week that scares me
- Book a massage twice a month as a treat for staying on track

Ultimate goal

Look in the mirror and see myself in the size 10 dress I wore at my cousin's wedding

Feel the sensation of my wedding dress fitting perfectly

Hear the comments from my friends as they all tell me how amazing I look

Relationship Success

First step

Join a dating agency

Have a makeover

Get actively involved in something I enjoy – like joining the local wine club

Decide what sort of partner I want, and write down what characteristics they must have

Success habits

- Look after my appearance
- Schedule times to go to places where I can meet people, e.g. galleries, adult education classes
- Do one unusual thing a month, like speed-dating

- Once a week, go out with friends
- Keep fit
- Read the newspapers and keep up with current affairs
- Practise dating conversations in front of the mirror or with my friends
- Chat online with people who have similar interests to me

Ultimate goal

To live with a partner

To be in a mutually supportive relationship

To get out of my current relationship and into one which will allow me to grow as a person

Running a marathon

First step

Buy a book on 'how to run a marathon' and read it

Work out a programme for running

Find a running club

Find a running partner

Book a session with a personal trainer

Success habits

- Run for x miles daily
- Follow the schedule and increase the length and duration of the runs
- Allow for time off to let my muscles heal and strengthen
- Eat healthy, nutritious foods
- Vary my routine so I stay motivated

Ultimate goal

Crossing the finishing line on (insert date) in (insert location)

Seeing photograph of me crossing the finishing line

To wake up the morning after the marathon and to reach out and hold my competitor's medal.

Career

First step

List what I want in my new job

Join a recruitment agency

Create CV

Success habits

- Research job options
- Review skills
- Go on an IT course
- Contact agencies weekly
- Read appointments section of appropriate trade paper/magazine
- Network
- Practise interview skills
- Research the companies I am going to be interviewed by

Ultimate goal

Getting the letter confirming the starting date and salary of my new job

To hear my partner cheer when I phone and tell him that I got the job

To see the look on my (soon to be ex-) colleagues' faces when I tell them that I am leaving

Fertility

First step

Go to medical practitioner and have appropriate checks

Success habits

- Eat properly
- Have fun sex
- Get on with life
- Book time for complementary therapy treatments
- Spend time learning about good nutrition
- Book time for romantic evenings
- Take time out to communicate with, and listen to, my partner
- Set a deadline – if it doesn't happen by …

Ultimate goal

To hold my healthy baby in my arms

To hear my newborn baby laugh

To see the look on my partner's face when he first sees our child

Writing a book

First step

Decide how long the book is going to be, work out how many weeks you are going to take to write it, and work out a plan of when in the day you are going to write

Buy any materials you need, and the *Writers' and Artists' Yearbook* as a guide to your steps

Success habits

- Write x number of words every day
- Go for a walk every day
- Do your daily self-hypnosis and work on the plot as you do so
- Do weekly research into your target market
- Send a letter per week with a book outline and the first three chapters to agents and publishers

Ultimate goal

To be standing in a well-known bookshop, next to a cardboard cut-out of myself, with a queue of people in front of me, waiting for me to sign my book

To feel my new book in my hands and smell the scent of new paper as I flick through the pages

Stopping smoking

First step

Pick a date to stop. Have your last cigarette and clear out your ashtrays, and get rid of any remaining cigarettes, ashtrays, lighters or matches

Success habits

- Sip orange juice
- Pinch your finger and thumb together to distract you at times when you would have smoked
- Reward yourself weekly with a treat
- Put the money you save into a jar

Ultimate goal

To become and remain a non-smoker

To see myself enjoying life without smoking, smelling fresh and feeling healthier

To see the money I used to spend building up in a glass jar in the kitchen and taking a holiday on the proceeds

Learning a language

First step

Find a course at night school

Go online and register with a language programme

Borrow a training programme from the library

Success habits

- Set time every day to work on the course
- Attend classes
- Buy newspapers in that language
- Find a radio/TV channel in that language and have it on in the background for half an hour every day
- Have one morning a week when I 'think' in that language

Ultimate goal

To go to the country for a holiday, and speak and understand the language comfortably

To hear myself speaking confidently to someone in a shop in that language

To read a Harry Potter in that language

Useful Information

Websites

The author's website
www.ursulajames.com
Ursula James and her specialist team can be contacted through the website for one-on-one sessions in becoming amazing. You will also find details of the 'Be Amazing' workshop. And hypnotherapy training courses for healthcare professionals.

www.authentichappiness.org
Test how happy you are via the Inventory of Strength self-reporting questionnaire.

CDs

Hypnotherapy CDs available from *www.ursulajames.com* or by calling 0845 055 9191

Candles

The success candle referred to on page 208 can be obtained from *www.ursulajames.com* or by calling 0845 055 9191

Books

Ursula James, *Clinical Hypnosis Textbook: A Guide for Practical Intervention*, Radcliffe Medical Press, July 2005

This is a manual for learning hypnotherapy and is required reading in eight UK medical schools including Oxford and Cambridge. It is available online from *www.ursulajames.com*

Maxwell Maltz Foundation, Bobbe Sommer (ed.), *Psychocybernetics 2000*, Prentice Hall Press, revised edition, 1996

Richard Layard, *Happiness: Lessons from a New Science*, Penguin Press HC, 2005

Daniel Goleman, *Emotional Intelligence*, Bantam Books, 2005